Leverage Your Expertise

16 Entrepreneurs Share Their Small Business Success Stories and Lessons Learned

©2021

Compiled by Alina Vincent

Leverage Your Expertise

LeverageYourExpertiseBook.com/gifts

Leverage Your Expertise

16 Entrepreneurs Share Their Small Business Success Stories and Lessons Learned

© 2021 By Alina Vincent

All rights reserved. No part of this book may be reproduced or transmitted in any manner or by any means, electronically or mechanically, including photocopying, recording, and/or retrieval system without prior written permission from the author, except in the case of brief quotations embodied in a review. For information, address Alina Vincent, Business Success Edge, 9732 Pyramid Highway, Suite 323, Sparks, NV 89441.

This book may be purchased for educational, business, or sales promotional use. For more information, or to order additional copies of this book, email Alina at Book@BusinessSuccessEdge.com.

All information written in this book is of relevant content and written solely for motivation and direction. No financial guarantees. All information is considered valid and factual to the writers' knowledge. The authors are not associated or affiliated with any company or brand mentioned in the book, and therefore do not purposefully advertise nor receive payment for doing so. All authors own their copyright to their story and original chapter. The authors and publisher do not assume and hereby disclaim any liability to any party for any loss, damage, or disruption caused by errors or omissions.

BusinessSuccessEdge.com

ISBN 978-1-7354408-2-8

Library of Congress Control Number: 2021944853

BONUS GIFTS

This book comes with free gifts, exercises, and resources from each of the contributing authors.

You can access all of them on the bonus Resources Page:

LeverageYourExpertiseBook.com/gifts

LeverageYourExpertiseBook.com/gifts

Leverage Your Expertise

LeverageYourExpertiseBook.com/gifts

Contents

Leverage Your Expertise... III

Introduction: The Myth: Working Hard to Make More Money
by Alina Vincent..3

Chapter 1: The Six-Figure Expertise-Based Business Framework
by Alina Vincent...11

Chapter 2: The Difference Between Growth and Leverage— Which Do YOU Want?
by Alina Vincent...37

Chapter 3: Saving Starfish
by Ian Foster..59

Chapter 4: Hiding in Plain Sight
by Huda Baak..75

Chapter 5: Pursuing Your Purpose with No Regrets
by Dr. Jane Cheng..91

Chapter 6: Make a Difference: Your Tribe Is Waiting
by Candas Barnes...103

Chapter 7: Showing Up for YOU
by Erin Arnold..119

Chapter 8: It Only Takes One to Start the Change
by Aneta Chencinski...133

Chapter 9: Awaken Your Authentic Voice
by *Diann Alexander* 143

Chapter 10: Find Your Divine Path and Live Your Purpose
by *Carmen Gélinas* 157

Chapter 11: Numbers Busy Business Owners Can Count On
by *Marie Gibson*..171

Chapter 12: Where Leverage Really Starts
by *Monica Bijoux*...185

Chapter 13: A Twitching-Eared Zebra on the Leading Edge of Change
by *Barbara Lawson*...197

Chapter 14: Unlock & Live Your Creative Dreams
by *Sam Whitesell*...213

Chapter 15: Dancing Through Life
by *Melanie Dale*..229

Chapter 16: You're One Action Away from Changing Your Life
by *Sidra Gaines* 245

Chapter 17: Always Go with Your Gut
by *Christine Grauer*...253

LeverageYourExpertiseBook.com/gifts

Leverage Your Expertise

LeverageYourExpertiseBook.com/gifts

This book is dedicated to all entrepreneurs who have shown resilience and dedication to their craft and continue to leverage their expertise, grow their business, and thrive even in the face of a worldwide pandemic.

Leverage Your Expertise

Introduction
The Myth: Working Hard to Make More Money
by Alina Vincent

I grew up believing you have to work *hard* if you ever want to make *more* money and get ahead.

And by "working hard," I don't just mean doing your job well (although that's important, too). I'm talking about putting in overtime at the good, well-paying job you already have, and/or getting a side gig (or two!).

After all, that's exactly what my parents did. Even though both of them taught at the university in Uzbekistan (one of the former Soviet Union republics), I remember them spending long hours after work privately tutoring students or taking on one-off projects. It seemed to be the norm in the society I grew up in—the more money you wanted (or needed) to make, the more hours you had to put in to make it happen.

No wonder I lived with this false belief for most of my life—that I had to trade hours for dollars!

No matter what else I had going on, I always had a second job or a side gig. For instance, while I was working as a lecturer at the university, I had multiple second streams of income (working evenings and weekends): tutoring, catering, translating, and selling stock photography.

As far as I was concerned, that was the only way I knew to make *more* money—by working more hours.

Eventually, I decided to turn one of my side gigs into a full-time business. I started a photography studio, and before long, I was generating six figures. Yay!

But without realizing it, I had built it on a foundation of that core belief—that I needed to work long, hard hours to achieve success.

So, of course, I hit the ceiling after just a couple years. I'd reached a point of having no more hours in the day available to make more appointments or to take on more clients.

Then, one day at a conference for new entrepreneurs, the speaker asked the audience to raise our hands if we would rather win a million dollars in the lottery than work to earn it. As you can imagine, nearly every hand went up. I was one of just a handful of people who wanted to work hard for that money.

I can still remember that moment… how everyone stared at me like I had two heads. Why wouldn't I want that money just given to me?

But no, not me—no sirreee! I had principles! I wanted my money to be earned, and I was proud of it. I literally didn't even want that lottery money unless I worked for it. Otherwise, in my mind, it wouldn't "count," and I wouldn't feel good about having it.

Can you relate? (Or is it just me, again?)

That was a huge lightbulb moment for me.

I spent hours replaying it in my head.

Why did I feel this need to work SO hard for my money? Why couldn't I allow the money to come "easy" to me? Why did I believe that I didn't deserve it unless I paid for it with my time? Why was I limiting myself so much?

And the most important question… what if things could be different?

What if I could create a business that wasn't based on how much time I put into it, but on how much value I brought to my clients instead?

What if success was not about the number of hours I worked, but rather my ability to use those hours wisely and maximize their potential?

What if "making more money" was not defined by how much I worked, but by how well I leveraged my time, gifts, and expertise?

After all, I could create any business I wanted!

It was an amazing epiphany. And it became the philosophy that defined my second business—the one I built on a foundation of leverage versus working hard.

The coaching business I have now has no ceiling. There is no limit to how many people I can help, how much money I can make, or how big it can grow. I've built it to scale easily by leveraging my time, expertise, knowledge, talents, and resources.

I started my new business by creating an online program. (If you haven't already, check out the first book I wrote in this series on how to do just that: *Teach Your Expertise: How to Grow a Business and Become a Success by Creating an Online Class or Program*.)

In retrospect, it's interesting (and *sad*) to examine the faulty thinking that affected my photography business. I was very clear to myself—I didn't want to build a BIG business—just enough to replace my previous salary of $40K per year, plus maybe a bit extra. According to my rationale at that time, if it took hard work and long hours to create a $100K business, it would be twice as hard to run a $200K business. And forget about a million-dollar business—just imagine how many extra hours and time and effort that would take!!! Why would anyone in their right mind want THAT?!

(Of course, a million-dollar business supporting thousands of clients is exactly what I have now, AND I work far less than I ever did in my photography business.)

When you have a leveraged business, it means you work smarter, not harder *(believe me, it's not a cliché)*, and you have the ability to create huge impact and income without sacrificing your time and trading hours for dollars. It means you can **spend less time supporting more clients**.

But it doesn't stop there.

You can leverage your connections, your resources, your circle of influence, your past experiences, your unique background, your team, your opportunities… really, there's no limit to what you can leverage to make your life easier.

And that's why I'm so passionate about this book. **Because the concept of leverage changed my life, and I want that for you**.

Leveraging my expertise allowed me to create a business that's now reaching hundreds of thousands of people and making an impact with entrepreneurs all over the globe. I've become friends with so many of the coaches and experts I looked up to when I first started out. In fact, many of them now seek my advice when it comes to leverage.

It allowed my husband and me to travel the world with our kids and extended family. We finally have that time and money freedom that draws so many people into entrepreneurship.

I am so grateful to be where I am in business and in life! And I want you to know that your dream is possible, too.

In the pages of this book, not only am I going to teach you the foundational principles of how to add leverage to your own business and the exact strategies I used to get where I am now, but you're going to hear from 15 of my clients who used my teachings and systems to leverage their own businesses.

Knowing how to leverage your expertise can be the key that gives you back your time and your life. *Take it from someone who has been there… and found a way out!*

Here is the bottom line:

Over the course of the last ten years, I created two businesses. Both have reached the six-figure mark in the first year and a half. After that, they evolved very differently.

I built the first business using sheer hard work, grit, and determination. Not only did it stop growing after reaching six figures, but I was exhausted and stressed. This business depended a full 100% on me showing up and putting in the hours. If I stopped working, the entire business would shut down, which also meant my income stream would cease to exist. All of my services and offers were based on a one-on-one model. It was not leveraged, it was not scalable, and it was not sustainable. I walked away from it.

I built the second business by leveraging my expertise. There is no ceiling to how much money it can generate or how many people's lives it can change. It's scalable, which means I can grow it as big as I want without adding any extra hours of my time or much of extra effort. It's based on creating leveraged online programs and a one-to-many model. And… if I take a vacation, the money doesn't stop coming in. That's the business I still enjoy today!

One of these is an *actual* business. The other was a J-O-B disguised as a business.

Which one do you think is more rewarding and fun to run? Which one do you think allows me to have real entrepreneurial freedom?

If you are ready to discover what it takes to create a leveraged business you love (and that loves you back), I'm so glad that you are holding this book in your hands.

My hope for you as you read is that you'll be inspired and informed… that you'll believe that your dream *is* possible, and that you'll discover practical strategies and methods for leveraging your time and resources, making a bigger impact, and of course, hitting that six- or seven-figure mark.

I, along with all of the entrepreneurs featured in this book, want you to learn from our journeys, success stories, mistakes, and lessons learned. We want to encourage you in taking the right action and fast-track your success in creating a leveraged, scalable, and profitable business based on your existing knowledge and experience.

And, as a BONUS, we also want to support you with a multitude of free gifts to uplevel your life and business based on our own unique expertise.

You'll find those gifts on the Resource Page, here:

LeverageYourExpertiseBook.com/gifts

Chapter 1
The Six-Figure Expertise-Based Business Framework
by Alina Vincent

It's time to roll up our sleeves and dive in! I hope you're feeling excited and motivated to discover the power of leverage in your business and your life (and ultimately, in the lives of the people you're here to help!).

As promised, I'm going to share with you my scalable business model and some very specific strategies my clients and I use to leverage our businesses.

However, I have to start by saying that I don't believe there is a single "right way" to success.

That's why I'll be showing you how you can create leverage YOUR way, without following a cookie-cutter approach *(who wants that, anyway?)*

Before we do that, though, let's look at the big picture of creating a successful six-figure business and beyond. What does it actually take to reach that mark? What are the most critical elements to have in place to make it happen?

After working with thousands of clients, I've put together a Six-Figure Expertise-Based Business Framework to answer those questions and more:

One of the most important things to understand as you study this framework is that *it's essential to have all five elements in place:*

1. Focus

2. Positioning

3. Platform

4. Product

5. Promotion

Ready to get to work?

Grab some paper and something to write with (or your laptop). We're going to walk through each of the five components of the Framework in detail; as we do, I'll give you some assignments to guide you in completing the inventory of where you are now. That way, you'll know what you already have in place and how to move forward for better results!

As you complete the assignments, remember that no one is going to see what you write. Be as honest as possible, so you have the clearest possible direction as you begin to implement what you learn.

1. Find Your Focus

Your focus is the core of your business, and that's why defining it is the first step.

Finding your focus means being crystal clear on what niche you want to serve—who is your ideal audience, and what specific solution do you want to provide for them?

In terms of a bigger picture, you might want to look at it this way: "What do I want to be known for?"

You might've already "named it and claimed it." If that's the case, congratulations! Defining your niche is one of the toughest first steps in creating a successful and profitable business.

The key here is to be as specific as you can be by identifying your *one* hot area of expertise and choosing one well-defined group of ideal clients you want to serve by solving a *specific problem* they have.

I know, I know… you might be saying, *"But I can help everyone,"* or *"But my method works for any person and in any situation."*

It's especially hard if you have a lot of special gifts and talents… when you can do so many things well, and you love doing all of them.

It feels like any time we narrow the scope of our offer by focusing on a specific audience or subset of our skills, we leave money on the table. It's tempting to keep our options open and not leave anyone out.

However, the opposite is actually true:

When we are trying to be all things to everyone, we are most likely not going to be of interest to anyone. While trying not to limit ourselves, we make it really hard on everyone around us to understand what we do, or to promote and refer us.

I know this from personal experience.

When I first started my photography business, I thought that the more options I offered, the more clients I would have. After all, I could help ANYONE with their photography needs. I offered packages for family portraits, commercial photography, engagement photos, glamour and boudoir sessions, product photography, senior portraits, etc. At one point, my website had 17 tabs covering the different types of packages I was promoting.

Yet I wasn't getting any traction. I didn't have a line of customers out the door wanting to work with me.

I was also attending a lot of networking events, where I would tell anyone who was willing to listen about the variety of cleverly named photography services I offered. But it didn't seem like anyone was interested in hiring me or recommending me to others. They seemed to forget about me as soon as they walked away.

Some of the people I met asked me if I did headshots. Headshots?! That wasn't even something I wanted to do, because it was so "basic." It didn't require much creativity. It didn't use all of the amazing skills I had. So I very often answered that I did not.

Yet I kept hearing that question again and again.

And finally *(ok, I'll admit it… it took almost six months!)*, it clicked. I realized that I was not listening to what my people wanted. I was not paying attention to what they were willing to pay money for. I was diluting my message by offering too many "creative" choices, and I did not see the "gold mine" that was right under my nose

Lightbulb!

So I made the decision to niche down and become known as the headshot photographer. I stopped offering and promoting everything else and focused specifically on helping entrepreneurs with their marketing needs.

Almost overnight, my business changed. Suddenly, when I talked about what I did, people paid attention. They leaned in and wanted to know more. I started getting recognized for the quality of headshots I created. Soon, daily referrals and inquiries about working with me became the norm. I was quickly becoming known as the "specialist"—the go-to photographer for business headshots.

Over the next few months, I became the highest paid headshot photographer in Reno, NV. People would even fly in from out of state to work with me. And that's what led me to breaking six figures and getting my calendar completely booked.

Do you see how success came only after I focused on *one* hot area of expertise and chose *one* well-defined group of ideal clients I wanted to serve by solving a *specific problem* they had?

That's why I'd like to challenge you to FOCUS *(we'll talk about how to do it in a much more scalable and leveraged way than I did in the next chapter).*

The truth is, when we focus on a specific niche or skillset, many more doors and possibilities open, which can very well lead to a successful and profitable business!

The more specific and focused you are, the easier it will be to stand out from the crowded market. The easier it will be to create a special hot-selling offer. The easier it will be to find the people who're looking for just what you offer. And the easier it will be to find the right strategy and words to market and promote it!

Now, it's time to get out that paper and pen. Answer these **5 Essential Niche Clarity Questions** for your business:

1. Who is your ideal client (gender, age, occupation, marital status, income, location, etc.)? What special characteristics does your ideal client have (education, lifestyle, life experiences, goals, behaviors, beliefs, values, personality traits, interests, etc.)?

2. What frustrates your ideal client about his or her current situation?

3. What are your ideal client's biggest obstacles or challenges?

4. What ONE thing does your ideal client want to have the most?

5. What specific programs or services do you offer that will get your ideal client the result he or she wants the most?

If you would like additional help with refining your focus, download my FREE step-by-step "Find Your Niche" worksheet here: LeverageYourExpertiseBook.com/gifts.

For right now, in order to keep moving forward, you can simply select *one* of your possible areas of expertise and *one* audience to focus on as you read (you can always adjust it later).

Assignment #1: Evaluate Your Focus

1. Write down your business' one main focus.

2. On a scale of 1 to 10, rate your level of clarity on your expertise, your niche, your ideal clients, and the specific solution you provide.

3. How well is it working for you right now? (How easy is it for your ideal clients to understand what you can do for them? How many clients do you have? How satisfied are you with your revenue? How do you feel about the quality of clients you are attracting? Etc.)

Let's now explore the rest of the **Six-Figure Expertise-Based Business Framework.**

Please note: The next four parts of the Framework (the four Ps) need to be developed and addressed in your business simultaneously. Think of it as a circular model; you need to expand from the center outward by growing and improving in all of these areas.

2. Positioning

Your positioning is how people see you. It's a combination of your visibility, credibility, influence, and authority that creates trust in you and your brand.

In most cases, positioning doesn't happen overnight (there are exceptions, of course: if you made an appearance on a popular national TV show, you could become an instant "celebrity" expert on your topic). In most cases, though, you build your positioning over time to become the go-to expert in your field.

Here are some of the different ways you can position yourself as the authority in your industry; choose the right one(s) for YOU:

- **Book.** Writing a book is one of the oldest positioning tools in the book (pun intended). Becoming a best-selling author gives you instant authority and positioning. Of course, writing an impactful book takes quite a bit of time and energy, and if you'd like to make money off it, you need a good monetization process.

- **Podcasts.** Start your own or become a guest on one (or several). Hosting a podcast is a proven authority-building strategy that allows you to share your message with thousands or hundreds of thousands of people simply by talking into a microphone. There are two different methods for building authority through podcasting: build your own platform by sharing your thoughts and message, or "borrow" credibility by interviewing people with more influence, more authority, and a bigger following than you currently have.

- **TV or Radio Show.** Create your own TV or radio show (it's easier than you might think).

- **Blog.** Start an authority blog to share your expertise and advice.

- **Social Media.** Build a page or channel on the social media platform where your ideal clients spend their time.

- **Summits.** Participate in other people's summits or create your own.

- **Articles.** Write articles for online and print publication to position yourself as the go-to expert in a specific industry.

As you can see, lots of opportunities exist to improve your positioning, and fortunately, you don't have to do them all. Choose the ones that seem the most enjoyable or impactful for you.

No matter which method you choose, one essential component of positioning is recognizing and owning your expertise and being able to share it with the world in a simple, clear, and concise way.

To do so, I like to use credibility statements.

A **credibility statement** is a powerful and concise one-sentence description of why you're an expert in your field and why people can trust you.

Here's an example:

"I use my skills as an award-wining instructional designer to help people create online programs."

This statement inspires more trust and showcases more of my expertise than, "I help people create online programs," right?

You can have multiple credibility statements highlighting various aspects of your expertise to use in different situations and with different offers.

For example, I can say, "As the creator of a million-dollar business, I help business owners grow and scale their businesses."

Again, compare this with a simpler statement like, "I help people grow and scale their businesses."

One more example: "I teach people how to create profitable programs and 5-Day Challenges, and we've had thousands of students complete our trainings and successfully implement our processes in their businesses."

All of these statements help position me as the trusted expert by emphasizing my experience, expertise, and credibility.

Now, you might be thinking...

"What do I say if I'm a newbie?"

If you're just starting out and don't yet have the results and accolades from working with lots of clients, emphasize what *you* have done. For example:

"I've been researching this topic for the past [amount of time], and I've created my own unique system to [result or benefit]."

"I've earned my certification from…" Or, "I have been trained by, [credible expert]." (I call this borrowing authority from your teachers and mentors.)

You can talk about the results and transformations you've created in your own life, or tap into your past careers or life experiences and tie in how they give you a unique skill set and approach.

For example: "I use my master's degree in engineering to help entrepreneurs create a systematic, logical, step-by-step approach to packaging and monetizing their expertise."

Let's spend some time thinking about your positioning.

Assignment #2: Evaluate Your Positioning

1. On a scale of 1 to 10, rate how well you're positioned right now in terms of authority, visibility, credibility, and being seen as the go-to expert. How much influence do you have?

2. What are you currently doing to improve your positioning?

3. Write down several credibility statements you could use to position yourself (keep each statement short and highlight just one credibility point in each).

3. Platform

Your platform is your access to people. It's *where* you share your message, *where* you connect with new ideal clients, and *how* you communicate with them. **Platform gives you permission to speak to a group of your ideal clients about your topic and solutions.**

A great platform empowers you to grow your influence and your following, and therefore consistently bring in new leads, enroll new clients, and fill your programs… by building connections and relationships.

That's why it's so important to ensure you're consistently growing your platform and gathering your ideal clients in one place—so that every time you make a new offer or launch a new program, you've got ideal clients lined up, warmed up, and ready to invest in your offers.

If one of your current struggles is knowing where to find people to fill your programs, or attracting new one-on-one clients, then chances are you haven't put enough attention on growing your platform.

Building an email list is, hands-down, the first and most important step in creating a successful platform. If you haven't started one yet, don't wait another minute! An email list belongs to *you*. And as such, it is a business asset that *you* control (unlike other platforms, like social media).

One major drawback to an email list, though, is that it's primarily a one-way communication tool that doesn't allow you to build an interactive community in the same way a social media platform might. While you can ask for replies, you're not as apt to get them, and your email subscribers can't communicate with one another at all.

In fact, this ability of your existing and potential clients to interact and engage with one another is one of the three crucial components of getting someone to say "Yes" to your offers online.

Over the years, I've identified the **3 Levels of Engagement** that must be present in your marketing to effortlessly convert your leads and followers into paying clients.

Level 1. ENGAGING WITH YOUR CONTENT

First, your ideal prospects need to engage with your content. It educates your audience, answers their questions, positions you as an authority, and builds trust in your expertise.

This can be done through your social media posts, emails, blogs, books, video content on YouTube, or live broadcasts. It could also happen through free digital downloads, like guides, templates, checklists, and infographics, as well as webinars, summits, workshops, and live events.

Level 2. ENGAGING WITH YOU

Second, your followers need to engage with YOU. They want to know and interact with the real person behind the digital profile. When you are providing opportunities for your ideal clients to engage with you, you take your offers and invitations from the "transactional level" into a long-term relationship-building level by supercharging that "know-like-trust" factor.

This can be done through interactive Facebook Lives, Zoom calls, workshops, discussions in the comment section of your social media posts, or live Q&As.

Level 3. ENGAGING WITH EACH OTHER

Third, you need to provide opportunities for your existing and potential clients to engage with one another. This is the most critical and often overlooked element of successful online marketing. Creating safe and supportive community environment gives your fans and followers a platform where they can share with like-minded peers their wins, successes, reviews, testimonials, and/or stories of transformation related to their experience of working with you. This social proof and "wisdom of the crowd" lead to increased trust in you and boosts the credibility of your business and offers.

I personally found that this can be done most successfully inside active and engaged Facebook groups. However, almost all social media platforms have elements of community interaction that you can leverage to provide a sense of community and belonging.

If you are struggling to get new clients online, you are most likely missing one or more of these critical levels of engagement (and most likely, it's the last one).

That's why, in addition to building an email list, I recommend using at least one community-focused platform, such as:

- LinkedIn
- Pinterest
- Facebook
- YouTube
- Instagram
- Twitter
- Clubhouse
- Meetups
- Podcasts
- Industry-specific forums or networking groups
- Your own blog

And here is one last important step when it comes to building your platforms:

Once you establish your community-based platforms, make sure you have a solid strategy in place to invite your followers to join your email list and vice versa—invite subscribers from your email list to interact with you on other platforms. This ensures that you are building your asset (your list) and establishing active communities where your people can talk to one another.

Now, let's spend some time examining the current state of your platforms.

Assignment #3: Evaluate Your Platforms

1. Write down the platforms you currently use (include everything from email to social media to professional networking platforms).

2. Next to each platform, write down the number of subscribers, followers, or connections you have.

3. How much time and effort are you currently putting into each of these platforms?

4. On a scale of 1 to 10, rate how successfully you're using each one to grow your following, communicate with potential clients, and attract new clients.

4. Product

Your product is the manifestation of the specific solution you provide to the specific problem your ideal clients want to solve.

Your product is what you are selling in your business *(that's how you make money!)*.

While your product could take many different forms, one thing is true—it will be unique simply because YOU created it. The unique value you provide within your offer comes from that special blend of your background, expertise, experience, skill, and passion. It incorporates your unique genius, your one-of-a-kind life story, your sense of humor and values, and your hard-earned knowledge and divine gifts.

For an expertise-based business, the most common paid offers include:

- One-on-one coaching

- Done-for-you services

- Done-with-you services

- VIP days

- Group coaching

- Retreats, workshops, and live events (in person or virtual)

- Memberships

- Masterminds

- Online programs

So, let's look at how your current paid offers perform *(in the next chapter, we'll do a deep dive into the most leveraged offer you could create in your business)*.

Assignment #4: Evaluate Your Products

1. Write down one or two of your main paid offers (the products you want to be known for).

2. On a scale of 1 to 10, rate yourself on how clear you are regarding the promise and benefits of your offers and the solutions you're providing.

3. On a scale of 1 to 10, rate yourself on how successful you are at selling these products.

5. Promotion

Promotion is a set of activities designed to take your potential client from Point A, the first point of contact, to Point B, where they invest in your product. These activities attract your clients' attention, create desire for your offer, and ultimately, lead them to buy.

The intention of any promotion is to increase the visibility of your products and services and to persuade and influence people to buy them.

As you can probably tell, promotion is a vital aspect of any business. It's also the one that causes the most confusion and frustration, because there are soooo many different ways to promote your offers.

Here are just some examples of promotional and marketing strategies you may be (or could be) using in your business:

- Email marketing

- Content marketing

- Social media marketing

- Relationship marketing

- Video marketing

- SEO marketing
- Webinars
- Challenges
- Live events
- Join ventures
- Referrals
- Speaking
- Networking
- Workshops
- Giveaways
- Summits
- Interviews
- Launches
- Automated funnels
- Paid advertisement

- PR

- And more!

Let's take a moment to look at where your business is now in terms of promotion.

Assignment #5: Evaluate Your Promotional Mechanisms

1. Write down all your current promotional tools and strategies, including those that are planned or in-progress (you could include things like upgrading your website, doing interviews, building a challenge, creating a lead-magnet funnel, hosting webinars, etc.).

2. On a scale of 1 to 10, rate your level of mastery of each of tools and strategies you wrote down.

3. How well are these strategies working for you? What kind of ROI are you getting from each? How well are they working for getting new clients?

Whew!

We just covered a lot of information, right?

I want you to reflect on where you are finding yourself now:

After reading thought this chapter and reviewing everything you are creating in your business, does it feel like that you're working *really hard,* doing *lots* of things and going in *too many* directions?

Does it feel like you should be getting better results based on everything you are doing, all the hours you are putting in, and the money you are spending on learning all these tools, platforms, and strategies?

You might be thinking…

"If I'm doing all the right things, how come it's so hard to fill my programs and get new clients?"

Or maybe your takeaway is that you are not doing enough. Just look at all of these options and ideas you could be focusing on!

If any of this sounds familiar, then you're in the right place.

What you discover on the pages in this book could save you thousands of hours and hundreds of thousands of dollars.

You are going to see why what you're doing right now may not be working for you and exactly what you can do to turn things around and finally create that six- or seven-figure business you dream of.

And it will empower you to share your message in a bigger way… and experience the excitement and freedom leveraged entrepreneurship can bring!

You'll learn specific and practical strategies for leveraging your expertise and scaling your business without spreading yourself too thin. You'll also read stories from my clients, so you can see what happens when you put these strategies into practice. You'll hear from a lawyer whose "work" no longer feels like work, a self-described "chameleon hiding in plain sight" turned highly visible, confident, successful entrepreneur who helps women take their power back, and a woman who experienced Divine Intervention while being held at gunpoint and then went on to live her Divine purpose, to name a few.

Each of them is sharing a special gift with you, too.

Follow the link below for a multitude of free gifts to uplevel your life and business:

LeverageYourExpertiseBook.com/gifts

Chapter 2
The Difference Between Growth and Leverage—Which Do YOU Want?
by Alina Vincent

I'd like to start this chapter by asking you a question:

Do you want to grow your business?

When I ask this question during live events and trainings, I get an overwhelming flood of responses: "Yes!" "Absolutely!" "100%!" "Of course!"

And I would bet your answer would be similar.

Well, this is a trick question.

And, as surprising it might sound, you actually DON'T want to grow your business.

It sounds a counterintuitive, right? I hope you'll hear me out.

When you *grow* your business, any time your revenue increases, your costs and operating expenses increase at about the same rate… which means that even as you generate more sales, the net income—the amount of profit your business makes—stays the same.

GROWING VS. SCALING

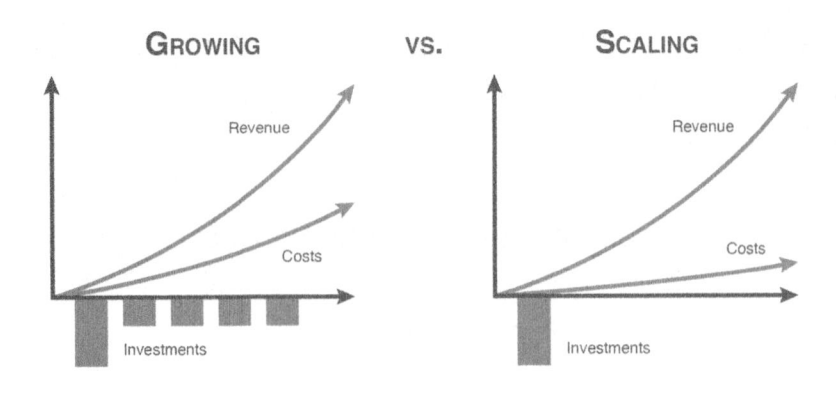

Growing chart: Revenue curve rising steeply, Costs curve rising moderately, with repeated Investments bars along the x-axis.

Scaling chart: Revenue curve rising steeply, Costs curve rising slightly, with a single Investments bar at the start.

Instead of growing your business, you want to scale it.

Scaling your business means that your revenue increases much more quickly than the cost of running the business.

Here's an example:

Imagine you're a coach who primarily works with clients one-on-one. This is a great way to provide value and transformation, but, when it comes to delivery, it's one of the least-leveraged business models out there.

Yes, when you enroll new clients and they pay you, your account balance goes up. But using the one-on-one model means that for every new client, you have to spend your time delivering coaching sessions (or pay one of your coaches to do it). That is the "cost" of delivering your coaching.

Your costs per client are fixed; with every new one-on-one client, the costs (time, effort, and money) remain the same and will not decrease as you add more clients. Plus, it's likely that you'll hit a "ceiling": a maximum number of clients your business can handle based on how many hours you (or your coaches) are available.

So, even as you grow your business, you're limited as to how much you can earn.

Let's look at a different business model:

Imagine that you create an online program. This one-to-many model empowers you to work with as many people as you like, while still investing only one or two hours of your time each week to deliver it.

This means that as you enroll more clients, your revenue increases while your costs remain the same (or increase only slightly)—more profit for you!

*The one-to-many model gives you a **leveraged delivery method** that allows you to scale your business indefinitely.*

Let's now look at a different aspect of your business: the enrollment process.

If you're currently using "discovery sessions," "strategy sessions," or any other type of free session to enroll new clients, then chances are you have to spend two or three hours talking with potential clients in order to get just one new client. And, if you're not great at enrollment conversations, it might take you five or even 10 hours of enrollment conversations to get one new client.

This means your cost of enrolling a new client is high in terms of your time—one of the most limited resources you have.

But what if you enrolled clients differently? Speaking from the stage in front of 100 of your ideal clients, or delivering a webinar to 200 potential clients, and then making your offer … you could easily enroll 10, 20, 30 or more people after just one 60-minute presentation.

As you can see, speaking from the stage or delivering a webinar **leverages your time** and is far more scalable than using one-on-one enrollment conversations.

As I mentioned in the last chapter, I learned some lessons the hard way. This was one of them.

When I started my photography business, it grew relatively fast. Within 18 months, it was generating six figures in revenue. Which was great, right?

It was… but everything I did was one-on-one or required my time; I worked with people in a studio, and then I spent time editing the best headshots of each client. Every new client meant I had to work more hours.

I was not leveraging my time. The only way to double my business was to work twice as many hours (and there were no more hours left) or to hire other photographers (which would have come with a large cost).

It was not a business I could scale, so I walked away from it.

And that's when I decided that the next business I created would be a business that could scale.

Now, I'm going to let you in on a big secret:

You cannot scale a business without leverage!

So what, exactly, is leverage? And how do you create it?

Here are my two favorite definitions of leverage:

Definition 1. Leverage is when you take a proven offer and shift your business model and systems so you can produce **similar results with less cost and less effort**.

Definition 2. Leverage is using something to its **maximum advantage**.

There are five main components—or pillars—of leverage. And the more strategic you are about recognizing and utilizing each and every one, the more scalable your business will become.

Pillar 1. Leverage Your Expertise. Your expertise is the unique blend of your background, skills, talents, education, divine gifts, and experiences. Your business should be focused on providing a solution that you are uniquely qualified to provide, because no one has the exact same expertise and experience. Therefore, your first boost of leverage should come from owning, expressing, and leveraging your unique expertise.

Pillar 2. Leverage Human Capital. Human capital is the influence and connections you already have. Consider the connections you've built and nurtured over the past five or ten years, and even throughout your life. Ask yourself, "How can I leverage my own connections and those of my network… people who trust me and know me as an amazing person? How much am I leveraging my relationships with my past clients and their referrals?"

Taking it one step further—how can you leverage the connections of your connections (think strategic joint venture partnerships and referrals)?

Pillar 3. Leverage Your Resources. Consider all the resources you already have in your business—time, money, team, technology. Consider how much time you spend on client-getting and money-making activities versus busy work that doesn't create a return on investment. Consider how much time and money you spend on new tools, programs, and trainings. Think about how you're using your team and the technology you've paid for. Are you leveraging them to their full potential? If you're investing time, money, and energy into any resource (including your team), but they're not creating a return for you, then consider eliminating them (or putting them to good use!).

Pillar 4. Leverage Your Achievements and Success. By celebrating and acknowledging all the things that are happening in your world—big and little—you can boost your credibility, authority, and positioning… all of which creates leverage. Infuse your marketing with the stories of your (and your clients') success.

Pillar 5. Leverage the Expertise of Your Mentors. There is no benefit to reinventing the wheel. No matter which field you're in or what type of business you have, someone has come before you. Someone has learned lessons the hard way, found solutions, and created success. Following someone else's proven system and investing in getting personalized feedback for your specific, unique business will shave years off your learning curve—and that's a huge component of leverage!

Now that you understand the five components of leverage, let's talk about the three keys to applying them in your business for maximum impact.

Key #1: You Must Have a Leveraged Offer.

A leveraged offer is one of the most leveraged pieces of your business, and the most important to get right. It's the first step toward leveraging your expertise.

A common mistake entrepreneurs make when they create a product, especially in the online space, is that they focus primarily on one-on-one clients. As you recall, I made that mistake with my photography business and quickly realized there was no way to truly scale my business with that model.

Here are some of the formats you could use for your offer in an expertise-based business (these items are listed in specific order from the least to most leveraged):

- One-on-one coaching *(the least leveraged)*
- Done-for-you services
- Done-with-you services
- VIP days

- Group coaching

- Retreats, workshops, and live events

- Memberships

- Masterminds

- Online programs *(the most leveraged)*

An online program, a true online program, is your knowledge, expertise, and experience on a certain topic that has been recorded and packaged in a way that makes it easy for people to access, consume, and use to get results… without any access to you!

Creating an online program is the absolute best way to leverage and showcase your expertise.

Here is another way to look at all of the different product options above:

Let's say you were fortunate enough to have a referral partner who said, "I'll bring you all the clients you want!"

That would be pretty amazing, right?

It would be, if your business was set up to scale.

If you're still in a one-on-one services, one-on-one coaching, done-for-you products, or VIP coaching business model, you can handle only so many clients before you run out of time in each week.

Imagine saying, "Please don't send me any more people. I don't have any more space on my calendar."

You wouldn't have to say that if you already had a leveraged online program. You could just add those unlimited clients into your program—without any additional work on your part.

So, what if you find that big lucky break and have an amazing joint venture or strategic partner, or your podcast goes viral, and everybody wants to work with you?

Will you be able to support them (and accept their money)? Or will you hit a ceiling where you have to turn people (and their money) away?

Offering a leveraged online program is the key in your ability to scale your expertise-based business!

When you have a program that can be taken at any time, day or night, delivering results without participants ever having calls with you, you have achieved that leveraged online program. Keep in mind, it's not meant to replace working with you; it's an opportunity for people to go through your process, step-by-step, in a home-study format.

(If you'd like more information on how to create an online program the right way, read my book, *Teach Your Expertise: How to Grow a Business and Become a Success by Creating an Online Class or Program* .)

Key #2: Simplify, Simplify, Simplify

Have you ever thought the reason you're not visible is because you aren't doing enough?

Or, that you're not getting clients because you're not using enough strategies and tools, or because you haven't mastered all of the hottest new marketing techniques and hacks? Or because you haven't created enough offers or programs?

You're not alone. Most entrepreneurs find themselves in this predicament at one point or another.

I don't know who started it, but there seems to be this notion in the business world that in order to be successful and make good money, you have to do everything and be everywhere.

So, entrepreneurs who are hungry to grow their businesses, change the lives of more people, and earn more money focus on too many strategies at once, spread themselves too thin, split their energy, don't stick to any specific strategy long enough, and create way too many products. They do this because they believe it will help them reach their goals.

In reality, it's completely the opposite.

The truth about success is that it requires focus and simplicity.

If you try to do everything I listed in the previous chapter (all the social media channels and all the different types of promotions and platforms), you're not going to make it. Trying to *do it all* is the main reason so many entrepreneurs end up overwhelmed and confused… and why they don't see the results they want.

When I first started my current coaching business, I fell into this trap, myself *(yes, this is another lesson I learned the hard way, and I'm writing this so you can avoid making this mistake!)*.

I created profiles and accounts on every social media platform I could find. Twitter, Pinterest, YouTube, Instagram, Facebook, LinkedIn, and even a few others that don't exist anymore. I built a website, started a blog, attended networking events, started writing a book, and did interviews.

Is your head spinning yet? Mine was: I spent hours each day creating content, repurposing it, searching for images, resizing them for various platforms, updating descriptions, and so on, just so I could "show up" every day on all of my social media platforms.

I was trying to do everything and be everywhere.

Eventually, I realized it wasn't sustainable for me, so I hired a virtual assistant to do all that busy work. I was no longer spending hours of my own time on being visible everywhere... but I was now spending thousands of dollars for my virtual assistant to do it!

Finally, about a year and a half into the business *(yes, it often takes me a while to learn!)*, I started tracking and looking at my numbers.

During one launch, I assigned a different tracking link to every single platform we were using (including press release websites, Google ads, and all of the social media platforms). We created 15 different tracking links to tell us where our traffic came from, where the hottest leads came from, and where people were actually buying.

The results were eye-opening to say the least (actually, they were shocking!).

More than 80% of the clients we got during that launch came from Facebook organic traffic. Yet I was spending hours and hours and thousands of dollars to be active on all those other platforms.

It hit me, then: my efforts to be everywhere and go in every direction (including paying to learn different marketing methods and systems and buying tools to get me farther, faster) were costing me dearly!

I was spreading all my resources—time, money, energy, creativity, focus, and attention—too thin. I thought the reason I wasn't growing my business as fast as I wanted was because I wasn't doing enough.

In reality, *I was doing too much.*

So I made a very big—and very tough—decision: I decided to simplify and streamline my business.

The most challenging part: deciding what to let go of.

As you're reading this, you may be thinking "Yeah, I like the idea of creating a streamlined, simplified, and profitable business. But how do I choose what to focus on? How do I know what's right for me, my business, and my clients, and what will result in the highest return on investment?"

I decided to look at my numbers to see where I was getting the best results… and I was able to let go of 90% of the platforms I was on *as well as* about 80% of the marketing strategies I was trying to make sense of.

Can you imagine how much this simplified my life?!

And guess what happened? My business started growing exponentially. In the next three years, it grew from around $100,000 to more than a million.

Now, I'm going to share with you a list of the questions I asked myself to determine what to let go of and what to keep (get out that pen and paper!):

- **What is my favorite way of expressing myself—communicating and sharing my message?** Consider writing, speaking on camera, speaking in front of a live audience, singing, acting, and creating visuals. Do I enjoy being in front of people? Do I enjoy sharing my opinions? Do I enjoy teaching or leading groups? Do I enjoy being interviewed or interviewing others? Do I communicate better through written word?

- **Where are most of my leads and clients coming from?** Take some time to look back over the past 10 months, the past year, or the past several years. Think about what's working for you right now. Have most of your clients come from networking meetings, one-on-one conversations, referrals, or Facebook Lives? If you don't have clients right now, consider where you're getting the most interest. Where do people lean in, ask more questions, and engage?

- **Which proven systems and processes have I already invested in?** Most likely, you've already bought a program or training that teaches a specific method, or you've invested time or money into a software, platform, or tool. It's worth focusing on what you've already learned or invested in; take that next step in practicing, implementing, and mastering the skills or tools you have now.

- **Which programs are selling the best?**

- **Which strategies are producing results for me right now?** Have certain methods resulted in more clients?

As a side note, I can't tell you how often I hear entrepreneurs say, "I just did a webinar and I got five clients from it!" and I'll say, "Great, awesome! Are you doing another one?" They respond with something like, "No, I'm now going to write a book/do an event/start a podcast."

I highly recommend that you stick to a strategy that's proven to work for you and spend time mastering it! You'll get much better results, much faster, if you aren't constantly moving on to the next shiny object.

Key #3: Find Your Lane and Stick to It!

Let's first review the Six-Figure Expertise-Based Business Framework that I introduced in the last chapter and its five components:

1. Focus
2. Positioning
3. Platform
4. Product
5. Promotion

As you now know, there are numerous options and pathways to promote, market, and position your business and offers.

And this is where the last key for maximum leverage comes in.

Pay attention—this is very important!

In order is to maximize and fast-track your results:

1. Choose **one** leveraged offer.

2. Choose **one** focus for positioning.

3. Choose **one** platform for promotions (in addition to an email list).

4. Choose **two** *or* ***three*** marketing strategies.

5. AND implement all of them for at least six months (or even better—for an entire year).

Sticking to your focus and your short list of marketing methods for an extended period of time is one of the hardest things for entrepreneurs to do! It's easy to get impatient when you have big goals for your business, which is why so many business owners try something for barely a week or two before moving on.

Here is the truth: you *must* stick to your chosen offer, positioning, platforms, and marketing strategies for at least six months (yes, even if you start losing excitement, even if you are not seeing the results right away, even if it feels "boring," and even if you come across a new-and-shiny idea).

Consistency and perseverance are critical… and what will get you to six figures and beyond.

When I made the decision to simplify and streamline my business, I decided to focus on just one platform: Facebook (and more specifically, Facebook Groups). You may remember that when I tracked my leads and sales for that one launch, I realized I was getting 80% of my sales from organic Facebook traffic.

It only makes sense, then, that I'd spend most of my time and effort there, nurturing followers, providing value, creating connections and relationships, and making offers.

Interestingly, Facebook checks off several of the items in the Six-Figure Expertise-Based Business Framework I outlined in the last chapter: in terms of **positioning**, as the creator of a Facebook Group, you're seen as the expert and leader simply because you lead the group; it's a **platform**, because it's where I build my community of followers and generate leads; and it's a great avenue for **promotions**—I get tons of clients through the 5-Day Challenges I offer multiple times each year in my Facebook group.

As you can see, I don't need separate platforms for positioning, list building, and marketing; I'm making **maximum use of a single platform—which is the definition of leverage!**

Facebook isn't the only game in town; several other platforms address several aspects of the Six-Figure Expertise-Based Business Framework. For example, podcasts give you positioning (credibility, visibility, and authority), and they act as a great platform, because they help you reach new people every week. Plus, you can use podcasts for promotion, to tell people about your free and paid offers.

I hope you are starting to recognize that there are multiple ways to achieve success. There are many paths to those six- and seven-figure milestones—you just have to find yours. And your path will be shorter and smoother if you stick to one leveraged offer, one platform, and a couple of marketing methods for at least six months.

For me, the winning combination of tools and strategies that got me to a million-dollar mark turned out to be doing 5-Day Challenge launches in my Facebook group with the support of joint venture partners to fill my online programs. I fully leveraged my expertise and experience through the online programs I created, and I kept my marketing and promotional strategies very simple and streamlined.

Now, it's your turn.

Answer these questions based on the assignments you completed in Chapter 1 and the new information I shared with you in this chapter:

1. Which leveraged paid offer will you focus on?

2. Which method will you choose for creating your positioning?

3. Which ONE platform will you choose for leads and relationship building (in addition to your email list)?

4. Which two or three marketing strategies will you master in the next year?

I hope that at this point, it's clear why leveraging your expertise and your business is the best way to create a sustainable and profitable business that can scale. And I hope you're beginning to see that there are many ways to leverage your business and reach your goals.

The bottom line is that *you'll be the happiest and most fulfilled if you create a leveraged business model that works for you*. As you explore your own formula for success, keep in mind each of the pieces of the Six-Figure Expertise-Based Business Framework (finding your focus, positioning, platform, product, and promotion) and the five pillars of leverage (skills, talents, education, and expertise; human capital; resources; achievements and success; and the expertise of mentors). When you do, you'll be empowered to scale and leverage your business as quickly as possible.

In the next chapters, you'll read stories from some of my clients who have used leverage to reach more people and increase their income (in many cases, exponentially). I hope that you'll find inspiration, and that by the time you finish this book, you'll feel equipped and empowered to leverage your business, increase your income, and enjoy the kind of freedom you crave.

And don't forget…

This book comes with free gifts, exercises, and resources from each of the contributing authors. You can access all of them on the bonus Resources Page:

LeverageYourExpertiseBook.com/gifts

Chapter 3
Saving Starfish
by Ian Foster

Remember the proverb about the kid who saves a starfish? In case you want to refresh your memory, it goes something like this:

A young child and her parents walk along a beautiful sandy beach after enjoying a picnic lunch, when a field of starfish comes into view. At once, the family notices hundreds of starfish lying on the beach, beginning to dry in the warm, early afternoon sun. The father says they must have washed up during high tide and been left behind. The mother, dismayed, expresses her sadness that so many starfish may perish. The young child, however, walks up to one of the starfish, gently picks it up, and walks knee-deep into the surf. She places the starfish back into the water with evident care, then returns to her parents' side. The parents, slightly befuddled, ask why she did this, pointing out that, quite obviously, the child cannot save all of the starfish. There are too many. There isn't enough time. They have other places to be and a schedule to keep. The child looks at her parents with a combination of regret and love, then tells them of course she understands she can't save all the starfish… but at least she saved that one.

My parents, like many, did their best with the tools they had. Sometimes they got it right, while other times they made mistakes. They made an effort to raise me with a heart for service, which I count among those things they got right.

My parents often used inspirational metaphors like the starfish story to instill values in me. They were careful to note that, while I couldn't help everyone, I could always help some.

These stories and proverbs had a huge impact on me. They reminded me to do what I could… even as they continually reminded me of what I could *not*.

Stories like that inspired me.

And stories like that limited me.

In our society, many things are said and done with the best of intentions. And despite sometimes having the intended positive effect, they also tend to have unintended effects, as well. The story of the starfish is infused with limiting beliefs that reinforce a scarcity mindset. Even as the positive aspect of those stories take root, so does the limiting.

I went on to work in politics supporting causes I believed in, and then attended a law school that trains heart-centered lawyers to build a just world. I went into government service as an attorney, working to stop those who would cause harm while protecting those who did good. Finally, I opened a private legal practice and pioneered the legal specialty of helping heart-centered business owners. Now, I specialize in making it easy for coaches, healers, and transformational leaders to find power in the law, so they can accomplish their missions with confidence.

That brief history illustrates the positive influence stories like the child saving the starfish have on others.

And yet, my potential to have an impact was limited by this notion that I can't help everyone. Many of us have learned to confront scarcity where it intersects with things like time and money, but stories like that of the starfish keep us thinking that scarcity still applies to how many people we can help.

Like all limiting beliefs, it doesn't have to be that way.

I knew my unique combination of experience, expertise, and skillset was needed in the world of heart-centered business owners. I was doing a lot of good by serving my individual legal clients. But when someone suggested that I expand my business and start coaching people on the law, helping them in groups through online courses, I scoffed. I told myself…

"I can't do that."

"Legal advice can only be provided one-on-one."

"If I'm not giving them true legal advice, I'm not really helping them."

"Nobody would pay what I would have to charge."

"If I don't teach well, I'll do more harm than good."

"The law is too complex; I can't turn that into a course people will understand."

"I can't serve groups and my individual clients."

"Doing legal work in your business is hard; lay people can't do it."

Does that sound familiar? You don't need to be an attorney to recognize the theme. When we deeply hold a limiting belief, we'll find excuses not to make things work. And those excuses feel as real as the ground under our feet.

The fact you're reading this chapter means you can guess how this story ends. Yes, I figured it out. I leveraged my expertise to educate and empower large numbers of heart-centered business owners in the law. With their new-found knowledge and confidence, my clients in turn go out and leverage their own expertise to help even more people.

This is proof you can leverage your expertise to become part of a ripple-effect of good work—and you can help more people than you think.

Quite frankly, if I can do it with a subject like the law, which is complex, surrounded by very real boundaries, and has tripwires for the unwary, then you can do it with your expertise, too!

But how?

Well, it may sound cheesy and simplistic, but I needed to get out of my own way. I needed to stop focusing on what *can't* be done and start focusing on what *could* be. I had to stop focusing on how *few* people I could help and start focusing on how *many*.

That renewed focus—along with the Alina's five pillars of leverage— helped me turn my passion for service and decades of experience into an online group program called **Legal Protection Made Easy**, which educates and empowers heart-centered business owners in the law, so they can confidently help their clients live better lives.

Take, for example, the first pillar of leverage: skills, talents, education, and experience.

Clients of my legal practice aren't simply paying for my time. They're paying for decades of learning an arcane subject, developing unique skills, and experiencing how the legal system works. So, the question became: how do I pass along that knowledge, skillset, and experience via a group program to help more people in less time?

I had to stop focusing on what could not be done. True, there are practical limitations in the law. I could not pass along decades of hard-fought experience in a couple months. I could not give people a license to practice law. I even could not give individualized legal services in the context of a group program. But what *could* I do?

I could boil down the law into the most important issues for heart-centered business owners. Those issues could be further narrowed into the handful of most important rules they need to understand and the handful of most important steps they could take on their own. And I could organize it all logically and make the information fun to learn.

The third pillar of leverage makes another great example: resources like time, money, and technology.

I used to focus on things I could not do. The limitations are real in that sense, but not real in that they don't have to stop me from serving more people.

I could not help hundreds of coaches and healers one-on-one with their legal problems. Not all of them could afford my hourly legal fees.

But I could leverage time by holding group calls to help many people at once. I could leverage finances by offering people value in a cost-effective format that is accessible to many. I could leverage technology by creating instructional videos that people watch at their own pace.

What about pillar number five: the expertise of my mentors?

I thought of my law school professors and my early supervisors in government. I was blessed to learn from people who were among the world's foremost experts in their subject matter, but who also knew how to teach.

This means I learned more from my mentors than just how the law works and how to make a difference. I learned how to pass on complex knowledge effectively and compassionately. When students take my programs, they see a lot of my law school professors and early supervisors in the way I teach today.

The five pillars are a great framework. But let's go beyond the theory now to see how leverage has transformed my life. Then we can see what leverage *really* means.

For that matter, what does a word like "leverage" actually mean?

It depends on context. My first career was in engineering, where "leverage" referred to things like lifting heavy objects. Then, in politics, "leverage" had what seemed like a different meaning, around making people do what you want. Later, as a government tax attorney who audited complex finances, "leverage" meant something else entirely, like using debt to expand opportunities or hide income from the authorities.

So when people recommended to me that I "leverage" my expertise through online programs, a lot of potential meanings flashed through my head.

Then I realized those meanings had a common theme: *using minimum effort to maximum effect.*

And that's when I realized what people meant by leveraging my legal expertise to help a much broader range of people... using my time and energy efficiently to make a bigger impact in the world.

It sounds obvious then, right? Why wouldn't I want to maximize the efficiency of my time and energy, so I can have a greater impact?

Well, it's not that simple when embracing assumptions that feel real but hold us back. So long as I believed I couldn't help large numbers and instead had to choose—a belief instilled in me with the best of intentions—I would sabotage myself by focusing on what I could *not* accomplish.

Before leveraging, my private practice traded hours for dollars. I spent time "butt in chair." It wasn't so bad. As an experienced attorney with a government background that gives me unique insight to address the most important problems facing business owners, I can make a good living in private practice. But it's also a lot of time and stress. Constantly making sure I have plenty of potential new clients who need (and can afford) individual legal work, meeting deadlines, spending all day in front of the computer… you get the idea.

I haven't abandoned my legal practice. I still provide private clients with the highest care. However, running online programs has enabled me to spend less time doing one-on-one work and helps me give individual clients VIP treatment. Group programs, in addition to doing real good, are a great source of income as well, so I don't rely solely on private practice. As a bonus, the programs drive clients to the private practice, so I don't stress over where the next client will come from.

This all works because the group programs are well-leveraged. Once the content is created and then modified based on feedback from the first couple of runs, the program can run repeatedly on the strength of that initial investment of time. Likewise, once the program launch is dialed in, it's a "rinse and repeat" sort of process.

At this point, with three online group programs established in law, taxes, and critical thinking, my "work" consists of free webinars, minor refinements to material, and running group coaching calls. I put "work" in quotes because those things don't even feel like work anymore. I love meeting people, learning about their needs, and helping them absorb a crucial subject. I foster a trusting, caring community of heart-centered business owners, so it feels more like hanging out with friends than anything I would call "work."

"Wait a minute," you're thinking. "You get paid to have fun and make a positive difference in people's lives at the same time?"

Yes. *That's* the power of leverage.

But the point is helping people live better lives. That's what my programs are designed to do.

If my clients' experiences are any indication, I'm succeeding.

Let's take "Jane" from Virginia:

Jane is a body worker and movement coach who was transitioning from employment to running her own business, helping people live healthier, more active lives. She wanted to set her business up the right way and make sure she was legally compliant. That would ensure its longevity and keep her free from unnecessary legal trouble. Jane also recognized that legal compliance was part of being in alignment with her values.

Jane joined Legal Protection Made Easy knowing very little about how the law applied to her business. She dug in, and among other things, learned about legal restrictions on coaching (there are more than you think), how to draft a viable contract in her own language, and how to set up her business properly.

After completing the course, Jane formed her own limited liability company, drafted the operating agreement, wrote her own terms for her courses, and even avoided falling victim to several scams designed to trap business owners who are not well-educated in the law. Jane would later tell me she felt calm and confident, knowing her limits and how to interview an attorney to do more complex work. That calm and confidence, Jane explained, was invaluable.

I often get asked how to get started dealing with legal issues facing a heart-centered business owner. The law can be complex and daunting, and it's understandable that a lot of folks feel anxious when thinking about it.

Well, my advice is twofold:

1. Don't let the anxiety stop you from taking action. I've seen too many instances of people who didn't set things up properly from a legal perspective because of anxiety, and the first notice they got of a legal problem was a subpoena, summons, or audit letter.

2. When you're ready to take action, find an attorney. Don't try and set up your legal foundation on your own. Online research and one-size-fits-all legal templates simply are no substitute for learning from an attorney who really knows what he or she is doing.

I have also put together a **checklist of questions to ask any attorney you're thinking of working with, to make sure that person is right for you.** Here are just a few:

1. What variety of experience do you have?

An effective attorney has a variety of perspectives. For example, I've worked in appointed political positions, government civil service, nonprofits, and private practice. Those positions instilled in me different perspectives that allow me to see all sides of an issue and remain open to learning and revising my beliefs based upon new information.

2. What's your legal specialty, and why did you choose it?

You don't want an attorney who is spread too thin among many specialties. You want someone who specializes in what you need and who chose it for a purpose that's in alignment with his or her own mission, not merely at random or to make a buck. For example, I chose to pioneer the specialty of legal issues pertaining to coaches, healers, and transformational leaders because I believe the world needs more people doing that work. It's in alignment with my desire to make a difference. The industry has multiple targets on its back, and I want them to stay in business, so they can help more people live better lives.

3. Do you offer cost-effective programs in addition to individual legal services?

You want an attorney who is not stuck in a rut—one willing to think creatively and who has worked to rid themselves of limiting beliefs that ultimately will manifest in their work. You want an attorney who can serve in multiple ways. Sometimes you'll need customized, individualized work. Sometimes you'll need to learn the issues, so you can make confident and well-informed business decisions. You'll need cost-effective ways of setting up your business properly. This is why I run a private legal practice where I give customized VIP treatment, as well as cost-effective coaching programs where I educate and empower people in the law.

Those are a few of the important questions to ask. You can get the rest by grabbing my gift below.

As far as creating leverage in your own business, my advice is threefold. First, think about your own limiting beliefs; pay close attention to whether you focus on what you cannot do rather than what you can. Second, use the five pillars as a framework to make more effective use of your resources. Third, don't delay in setting up a solid legal foundation. Legal problems don't go away when you ignore them. The longer you go without addressing the law, the more complicated and expensive your legal issues will get, with bigger consequences for small missteps.

All of this might seem daunting, but I promise: it's worth it.

***

Through his private legal practice and empowering group programs, Ian Foster is pioneering the legal specialty of helping heart-centered entrepreneurs serve the world with confidence by being in alignment with the law. Ian passes on his "inside knowledge" from 18 years of experience as a government business and tax attorney, breaking it down into understandable and actionable chunks, so you can build a long-lasting business with confidence and peace of mind. Learn more about Ian here: www.northbaybusinessattorney.com.

Get Ian's free gift ...

Ten Questions to Ask an Attorney Before Your Hire Them to help determine whether you've found the right attorney to help you set up your legal foundation properly, here:

LeverageYourExpertiseBook.com/gifts

Chapter 4
Hiding in Plain Sight
by Huda Baak

I believe in three things wholeheartedly:

Every woman deserves to be seen for who she truly is.

Every woman has a right to express herself fully, in all her glory.

Every woman has a gem within her that she longs to share with the world.

Sadly, too many women go through life not being seen, unable to express themselves fully, and hiding their gifts and talents. I know this because I was one of them.

Growing up in the Middle East, I was told I couldn't do certain things. My earliest memories were that I wasn't allowed to express myself, which resulted in my feeling like I had no voice. I was told to sit quietly, look pretty, and be compliant. I was hushed whenever I felt upset, disappointed, or God forbid, showed anger. Only happy feelings were allowed to be expressed.

Despite having progressive parents and a mother who was a pioneer in many ways across numerous cultures, when it came down to it, we very much lived in a patriarchal society where men ruled, and women followed. When I was told not to do something, I was a "good girl" and obeyed without question.

But now, things have certainly changed!

After working quite intimately with over 850 women from different countries, I can say with confidence that this patriarchy continues to exist regardless of where women were raised or their cultural background. Whereas patriarchal practices are overt in certain cultures, here in the United States, it's more covert—still, most every woman can speak to its presence.

By the ninth grade, I'd attended nine schools in several countries and learned multiple languages. This would've been challenging for any child, but for a quiet, introverted, young girl, it was excruciating. I desperately wanted to fit in, but I just couldn't. Not at first, anyway. Either I didn't speak the language initially, or the habits and the styles were so different from what I was used to that I was often left out and forced to fend for myself. And just as I'd get to the know the kids and school customs, it was time to pack up and move to yet another city and school. This happened nine years in a row.

What I learned from that chaos was how to become a chameleon and hide in plain sight.

I mastered the art of the chameleon, and I was proud of it!

To make things even trickier, my parents had a contentious relationship, and by the age of 10, I was put in the therapist position. Naturally, as many empathetic children do, I internalized their hostility and thought it was my fault. What I didn't know at the time was that most children growing up in these situations either go rogue and start acting out and getting into trouble, or they choose to take control.

In order to keep any semblance of peace in the house, the only real control I felt I had at the ripe age of 10 was to be perfect. If I were the perfect daughter and cleaned the house and did the laundry, then they would be happy and stop arguing. If I got straight A's and didn't ask for anything, there wouldn't be any reason for them to fight.

Unfortunately, no matter the level of "perfection" I achieved—even graduating as valedictorian—there would be no peace in that house.

Becoming a chameleon and a perfectionist required skills I've developed that served me well. Too well, actually, because they stuck with me most of my life and have been hard to break.

As an image consultant for the past 30 years, I've seen my share of women who have some version of this chameleon affliction.

Where we get into trouble is by wanting to fit in so much that we lose pieces of ourselves and forget who we really are. Much like tofu, we tend to take on other people's styles or mannerisms. Tofu is bland on its own, but takes on another flavor when blended with other vegetables.

I didn't want to be tofu anymore. I wanted to have my own, unique flavor!

Of all my habits though, the toughest to break was the quest for perfection. I had perfected my image. Not that I *looked* perfect by any stretch, but I had the image down. I knew the colors, styles, and shapes that looked best on me. That was a piece of cake! I'd grown up around beautiful, high-end European designer fashions, so creating a unique and authentic style for anyone on any budget was easy for me.

Yet even though I knew how to dress to attract the right attention and get the results I wanted, there was one key element completely missing: my inner game wasn't supporting my external image.

I might have looked great on the outside, but inside, I felt like a fraud. All the compliments in the world wouldn't sink in, because no matter how beautiful the facade, it is only a thin layer masking ugly truths.

Who was I to be teaching alignment when I wasn't completely aligned? How could I guide women on the right image for them when I was still playing small and felt as though I was hiding? I realized I had reverted to the little girl who was told to sit quietly, look pretty, and be compliant.

Fast forward many years and tens of thousands of dollars later, I got closer to finding my answer. I worked with gurus and healers from Tibet and India and a dozen mentors and coaches in Canada and the US. I kept searching for answers from people outside of me, and, although each person I connected with helped me in his or her own way, it wasn't until I connected with *my own source* that I got my answer.

Just like in *The Wizard of Oz*, it was in me all along.

That was one long and expensive lesson!

Next, I knew my business needed to evolve as I had, but I just didn't know how to do it.

It wasn't until I was in a car accident and spent a few months in literal darkness, shielded from light, sound, and motion that I was forced to be still. And without external distractions, it's much easier to tune in to our own spirit and hear divine guidance.

As frightening and lonely as it was, I gleaned tremendous value from being in that valley. It was in the many months of healing from the trauma that I forged a deep connection with my own source and finally listened to my inner wisdom.

It took me a couple of years to recover from my accident and feel comfortable working with clients again. But I listened to my guidance and decided to modify my work and focus to work with women on both the inner *and* outer aspects of their image. After all, hundreds of clients can't be wrong: **when the inner and outer are aligned, magic happens!**

I'd known for 10 years that working on the external aspects of image alone was no longer enough. I loved it, and I was highly skilled at it, but it was time for a change. So, after getting incredible results for hundreds of women in my professional experience, I felt confident in my gift of making any woman look and feel beautiful inside and out. Even the women who came on stage for quick five-minute makeovers stepped off feeling more uplifted than when they walked on.

So, I started looking at ways to leverage my 30 years in the image industry by learning to create an online program.

I had always wanted to, but thought that it would be impossible to create a visual business online. As a speaker, I got paid to travel and present on visual image. Audience members would come on stage so I could demonstrate various styles and how adding a touch of color here or an accessory there would completely up-level their look in five minutes or less. How could I do that virtually? How was I supposed to shop and go through someone's wardrobe online? It would be ludicrous! But then again, was it?

Here's what I learned:

Just about anything can be transformed into a virtual platform with proper planning and guidance. I shifted my perspective and looked at my current presentations objectively. What did my clients want?

That's when I realized that there were key elements that could in fact be modified to work online!

I took the systems that I used with clients both in my one-on-one consulting as well as on stage and tweaked them. I asked the same questions to prep my clients before we worked together, and I showed specific images to convey my key points. Then, instead of using live participants as models and physically bringing a rack full of clothes to my workshops, I showed the same clothes via an online presentation! It wasn't exactly the same, but it worked.

So, I took the plunge and created my first online program: **Power Up Your Presence to Get More Visibility and Authority!**

And as I write this today, my only regret is having waited so long to launch it. It took me a few months to get on board and figure out the mechanics and technology of it, but it was an eye-opening experience. I loved the creative aspect of it, too, and it came together better than I had expected!

Im so glad I didn't let my fears and objections stop me. For example, because of the nature of my work and how intimate it can be, I thought women might not feel as safe opening up online as they do in person with me. But I was pleasantly surprised. The women connected well, felt safe enough to share in the group, and were very encouraging to one another, which was remarkable!

I also found that recording my presentations was more difficult than I had first expected. I was used to speaking to live audiences with lots of interaction, so recording by myself into a computer felt strange! Dividing the talks into five-to-eight-minute segments was also a new experience, and it made me look at speaking in an entirely new way. By the third module though, it felt like I'd been creating online courses my whole life!

Leveraging my expertise online was a natural next step for my business. I'd spent 30 years speaking and doing one-on-

one image consulting, and as much as I love working with my private clients, it wasn't a sustainable business model. There are only so many hours in a week!

This program became a great entry-level offer for people to get valuable information for a relatively low price. They get to know who I am, so they can decide afterward if they want to work privately with me.

Before my accident, I had been a regular guest on a San Francisco Business Talk radio station during the commute time, but without an entry level offer, I wasn't able to capitalize on all that radio prime time. I had a blast talking and answering people's questions, but unfortunately, it didn't translate to money for me. But now, it's so much easier to sell from the stage or from an interview, because I have something to offer for a far smaller investment.

The biggest bonus of creating my program is that it made it so much easier to get clients and referrals. I was surprised when a couple of ladies encouraged their friends to join even before they had taken the course themselves! I had more people in my pilot than I had anticipated and loved every minute of it.

It also boosted my confidence and visibility and gave me instant credibility during interviews and while talking to new prospects. The best part is that I was able to leverage the connections with my extended friends and colleagues after a four-year absence while I was recuperating from my accident.

All in all, I'm so thankful that I accomplished what I had wanted to for so long but didn't know how to begin!

Perhaps best of all, it helps me get phenomenal results for my clients.

For example, Sheila was promoted to school principal within six months of us working together after being shut down for three years. Mary was offered a job in her industry exactly 10 days into our working together after being unemployed for 18 months. Carol landed her dream coaching client after working with me for two months. And Judy went from relative obscurity at a Fortune 100 company to VP in a few short years, and credits me with her confidence and meteoric rise.

It is not my intention to brag—in fact, it's quite the opposite. My mission is to get women (and girls) to take back their power, and to remember that as women, we are more powerful, more competent, and far more resilient than we were taught to believe. My passion is reminding women of their immense value and expertise, so they can stop dimming their light and playing it safe.

Each of the clients named above reached their dream job or ideal clients once they believed they deserved it and matched their inner resolve with the outer expression of that stronger sense of self. It's the *combination* of feeling confident and looking the part that's most powerful.

To help them do so, I developed a system that looks at image from four components: physical, mental, emotional, and spiritual: physically, how we *see* ourselves; mentally, how we *think* about ourselves; emotionally, how we *feel* about ourselves; and spiritually, how *connected* we are to our spirit and sense of self-worth. When all four aspects are aligned, we feel more beautiful and empowered, and we attract the right clients to us effortlessly!

Sarah's story illustrates this inner vs. outer game of image. At 22, her mother told her that she'd "never amount to anything"—that nobody would ever pay to work with her or listen to her, and that she needed "to become a secretary and get a real job." And so, at 58 years old, she struggled with feeling inadequate and didn't value herself despite the external appearance of success.

Sarah dressed well and was a successful entrepreneur, but she'd always struggled with her value and charging enough for her work. Underneath her success, she was still the child who'd been told that she wouldn't amount to anything.

This negative loop had been running her life and affecting her work, finances, and relationships for years. Once she learned about the mental aspect of image and became conscious of the underlying negative thought process, she realized how much she'd suppressed for years.

Sarah learned to reframe her mother's harsh words, so whenever the negative thought surfaced, she countered them with a true statement about who she is now—not as the scared young woman. Today, Sarah is happier, more engaged, and has in fact lost more than 25 pounds!

It's amazing how much carrying unconscious burdens affects our image, both inside and out.

Now, any good stylist can work on the external appearance by updating a wardrobe and choosing the right colors and styles. That's the easy part! The challenge lies in what's beneath that: The Authenticity Factor.

And that's why I named my business Authentically You Image Consulting. The focus is aligning who you are inside with the way you express it on the outside. It's about showing up in the world authentically, without pretense or a facade.

The first steps to creating the look and the life you want is to become conscious of the image you're currently projecting.

If you're interested in that awareness, I'd like to share the following quick exercise with you.

Exercise: Who Are You, *Really*?

Step 1: Get a pen and paper, and write down your answers to the following questions.

- Do you like the way you look?

- Are you happy with your style of clothes, hair, and/or makeup?

- If you could change anything about your look, what would it be?

Now let's dig a little deeper. As women, we tend to bend ourselves to fit the expectations of those around us. With that in mind…

Step 2: Reflect on and answer the following questions:

- Are you who you want to be, or who everyone *expects* you to be?

- How do you want people to see you?

- How do you want to be remembered?

Answering these questions helps you discover not only who you are now, but who you are *becoming*.

Overall, I loved the experience of not only creating my first online program, but in sharing it with so many women. Like many of you reading this, I too have a gem I long to share with the world, and I'm not hiding my gifts and talents anymore! I will continue to speak and remind women that we are amazing, powerful, and beautiful, no matter our size, shape, or ethnicity. It's time for each of us to tap into our inner essence and express it to the world!

***

Huda Baak is a leading expert on professional image and personal brand. For the past 30 years, she's personally worked with more than 850 women and has spoken before thousands more. She has appeared on numerous televised business talk shows and was a regular guest on Business Talk Radio programs in the San Francisco area. Her work incorporates a global perspective having lived and worked throughout the Middle East, Europe, Canada, and the US.

Huda is a champion for women leaders who want to grow their business, build more influence, and communicate with confidence. You can learn more about her here: www.HudaBaak.com.

Get Huda's free gift …

The 1-Minute Closet Makeover eBook to discover a 10-step system for decluttering, sorting, and evaluating everything in your closet to create a fabulous and functional wardrobe, here:

LeverageYourExpertiseBook.com/gifts

Leverage Your Expertise

Chapter 5
Pursuing Your Purpose with No Regrets
by Dr. Jane Cheng

I've always been passionate about helping others. That desire was the North Star for my career path: it led me to become a doctor, pastor, and later, a psychotherapist and coach.

I started my psychotherapy and coaching business because I know what it's like to struggle with finding direction, professionally and spiritually… and because I've come to realize how many people die regretting they didn't respond to their calling from God to live their purpose.

My journey began on a path that would bring me to the world of medicine. I went to medical school and then worked in a hospital providing healthcare services to those who needed physical healing.

But as so often happens, life showed me that being a doctor wasn't my true calling.

I received so many compliments from my patients about the way I motivated them and helped them feel better emotionally that I quickly realized medication isn't the solution to healing all problems.

While I went back to school to earn advanced degrees (a master's and a PhD) in healthcare to improve my services in the traditional healthcare setting, I also felt God calling me to work as a spiritual teacher and pastor (I'd felt this calling since I was a child, but this was the first time I pursued it).

I earned a master's degree in divinity, and while working as a senior pastor for several American churches, I also studied for my doctorate in divinity. As I transitioned my career, I experienced levels of stress commensurate to the amount of tuition I paid (I've invested more than a million in my higher education!). I knew the stress was simply a signal from God that I needed to equip myself to become a better version of me, so I could help more people.

So, I learned as much as I could about money mindset, determined to earn more while reducing my financial and emotional stress.

My goal? To live a balanced life!

For 25 years now, while continuing to work in the traditional healthcare setting, I've also worked in a ministry as a spiritual mentor.

One of the spiritual services I've provided is working as a chaplain at several hospitals, to support people who are dying and their families. That's where I found the path I'm on now.

So many of the patients who were dying regretted that they hadn't responded to the purpose, or calling, God laid out for them. I remember people crying as they told me they wished they'd lived their lives differently.

Meanwhile, I was also working as one of very few Asian female pastors in the southern United States… and I was facing many challenges as I preached to thousands of people.

I sensed a strong need to promote mental health healing for my church members and community residents.

Two desires—to help people find and live their calling, and to promote mental health healing—led me to study psychotherapy and, later, coaching. I earned two professional degrees and became a certified coach.

And I was absolutely driven to help more people be happier and healthier by creating a life and business according to their unique gifts.

I wanted to work with spiritual entrepreneurs on everything they needed to do that, from money mindset to finding and living their purpose.

For more than 15 years, I ran my business, Care and Counseling Coaching Center, Inc. (CCCC), offering psychotherapy and coaching services in a one-on-one model. That's the traditional model in the healthcare setting, and it's the one I knew when I started my business.

I worked *really* long hours. In addition to meeting with individual clients, I completed documentation and reports for each of them.

To put it simply, I was exhausted. And because I didn't have time for myself and my family, I burned out.

The worst part: I started to lose passion for my work. Plus, I knew that with the business model I was using, I could never grow or scale my business (or my income). I simply didn't have enough hours in the day.

I'd seen other entrepreneurs use a more leveraged business model: offering group coaching or online programs. And I knew that the only way I could continue helping others was to leverage my time and energy.

I knew I wanted to create an online program, but wasn't sure how. I didn't have the guidelines (or encouragement!) needed to take action.

I sought mentorship through Alina's Rising Stars Mastermind, and then, I created my first five-week group program, **Mission to Money Program.**

Naturally, I was able to work fewer hours while serving more clients!

Over time, I added leverage pieces: I created a weekly call to invite people to join the program (rather than doing one-on-one calls) as well as online modules to empower people to study on their own time—which meant I didn't need to teach the content live. I felt so relieved!

The results have been wonderful: I am making a bigger impact on others while being able to spend more time with my family. I have more time freedom and more energy! Plus, I've boosted my income. My pilot program made me $8,000. Just three months later, I ran it again after increasing the investment level and brought in another $16,000!

My confidence has increased, too. I know I can continue creating group programs, helping more people, and making a big impact, which feels absolutely amazing.

Now, I'm living my mission: to empower entrepreneurs to have the courage and boldness to play big—to step into their vision and dreams—by creating a business aligned with their soul purpose.

When they do, they can double their income while using their gifts to transform the lives of more people!

I'd like to share with you a few examples of clients who have used my teachings to do those things (to protect their privacy, I've included their initials rather than full names).

Through my Mission to Money program and Money Mindset class, one client, CT, changed her money beliefs, received healing, and created an abundant money mindset. The result: she doubled her income within a few months.

When another client, VV, came to me, she believed she couldn't invest in herself, and she worried often about money. Through our work together, she was able to change her spiritual beliefs. Now, she more than believes she can invest money in her personal growth—she does so! She's developed an abundant money mindset and created a business that aligns with her soul purpose. Within three months of working with me, she doubled her income—and created the life she desired!

KN came to me with a long family history of scarcity mindset. Through my program, she was able to receive healing and create a new identity and a clear message about her services. She attracted more new clients, and within six months, tripled her income. Even better, she feels like she's living her soul purpose!

Finally, after working with me, AA used his gifts and talents to create a second business he not only loves, but that is transforming lives… his clients' and his family's! Now, he is leaving a legacy he's proud of.

The one thing all these clients have in common is that their progress took off after they got clear on their unique gifts and their message.

Which is why I recommend that spiritual entrepreneurs who struggle with their message focus on their own unique gifts and strengths. Doing so will save you so much energy, and you'll be empowered to build your business with ease in a shorter period of time.

If this resonates, I'd love for you to try the following exercise, which is designed to help you get clear on your unique gifts and strengths, so you can create a business that aligns with your soul purpose (and this clarity will give you the confidence to position yourself as an authority in your field).

Exercise: 5 Steps to Get Clear on Your Unique Gifts and Strengths

Step 1. Write down your education and work experience. What you've done and what you've studied play important roles in the direction you choose to take your business. That with which you're already familiar provides a strong foundation as you move forward.

Step 2. Write down positive comments you've received from others that confirm your unique gifts. Often, our gifts come so naturally to us that we don't even realize they're gifts! Think about comments you've heard repeatedly from friends and family members and capture them on paper.

Step 3. Write down skills you have that you would also like to teach to others. Be open-minded! Again, you may not recognize your skills without some deeper thought, because they come naturally to you. Write down everything you can think of.

Step 4. Meditate to envision how others will react to your chosen topics. With your potential business idea in mind, consider how many people will be searching for your expertise as a solution to a problem they're having. Close your eyes and imagine your future vision, as well as the people you could help with your gifts and skills.

Step 5. Decide on the specific topic around which you want to position yourself as the authority. Once you're clear on that, you can begin to craft your business with the confidence that the process will be streamlined and successful.

These five steps will help you get clear on your purpose or calling and begin crafting a business around it. It bears repeating: the more clarity you have, the more quickly and easily you'll be able to reach your business goals.

Of course, being clear on your purpose or calling is also a powerful first step in creating leverage in your business, too.

I've found that developing that clarity has truly empowered me to position myself as the authority to teach people the money mindset necessary for them to create a successful business. And creating an online program has helped me build my community, create a signature program, and make more money!

Because it's my passion to help entrepreneurs live their purpose and earn more money, I'd love to now share with you some advice as I reflect on the program- and leverage-creation process I experienced.

I understand what it's like to struggle financially, and to feel like you don't have the money to invest in personal or professional development programs. However, I also believe (and have seen, in so many cases) that when you motivate yourself to find more resources and invest in yourself, you'll be able to use your unique gifts and talents to serve more people… and you'll receive more financial blessings from those people while you make a big impact on this world.

Your people are out there! They're waiting for you to share your wisdom and life experience. I can't emphasize enough the importance of pursuing personal and professional development; finding the right mentorship and guidance for you provides you with the clarity, encouragement, support, and systems to create and leverage a business around your unique gifts.

Don't worry too much about the technical aspects of leveraging your business. Focus on your gifts, and get the help you need to deliver them to the people who need them. You'll save so much time and energy by hiring and delegating the technological tasks that fall outside your unique genius area!

As I mentioned earlier in this chapter, as a chaplain, I've heard from many people on their deathbeds who wish they'd lived differently—that they'd pursued their purpose. My biggest wish for you, then, is that you listen to your calling and pursue your purpose.

Getting clear on your unique gifts building your business around them, and then leveraging your time, energy, and money, is hands down the most effective way to do that. Start today. You won't regret it.

***

LeverageYourExpertiseBook.com/gifts

Dr. Jane Cheng is a gifted healer and success coach who helps people create their businesses by using their unique gifts, which allows them to align with their soul purpose and transform the lives of many people. She has invested more than a million dollars in personal growth and professional education and earned four master's degrees and two PhDs in medicine, divinity, psychology, and business. In addition to her work as a coach, Dr. Jane has worked as an ordained pastor. She integrates all her knowledge and life experience to bring holistic healing and to coach people to double their income while living their soul purpose. You can learn more about her here: www.liveyourbestpurpose.com.

Get Dr. Jane's free gift ...

The Healthy Money Relationship Quiz to identify and repair problem points in your relationship with money, here:

LeverageYourExpertiseBook.com/gifts

Leverage Your Expertise

Chapter 6
Make a Difference: Your Tribe Is Waiting
by Candas Barnes

"If there's a book that you want to read, but it hasn't been written yet, then you must write it."

~ Nobel Laureate Toni Morrison

I didn't know it at the time, but getting fired on the first official Dr. Martin Luther King, Jr. holiday proved to be one of the best things that could have ever happened to me.

I had no idea what the future held when I dropped out of college with a 1.82 GPA a few months before getting fired. Because I needed work, I registered with several temp agencies. One sent me to a part-time job at Gallaudet University—the world's only liberal arts university for Deaf and hard-of-hearing people. That part-time job at Gallaudet Interpreting Service (GIS) gave me a glimpse of how I could use my natural gifts of communication, curiosity, flexibility, gregariousness, leadership, independence, and resilience in a career with unlimited possibilities.

After some research into the profession, I set my sights on becoming a professional American Sign Language (ASL) interpreter. I had no way of knowing I would eventually become one of the country's most well-known and sought-after interpreters. The career I have had still makes me pinch myself sometimes, and knowing how blessed I've been makes me deeply committed to sharing my career and paying forward all that I can to the next generations.

The quote by Nobel Laureate Toni Morrison at the beginning of this chapter has inspired me to do many things, including becoming an interpreter. In 1987, I discovered that Washington, DC, also known as "Chocolate City" because its population was over 80% Black, had a scant number of Black interpreters. I knew if there were so few in DC, there probably weren't many anywhere. I also knew my work was cut out for me since I didn't know ASL, had no connections in the Deaf community, and was a secretary. I would have to work hard, leverage relationships, and get people to buy into my dream.

I was again inspired by this quote in the fall of 2020. After being frustrated for nearly the entire 31 years I spent as a professional interpreter by the challenges systemic racism and other disparities created for Black Deaf people and Black interpreters, I knew it was time for me to "write the book"—i.e., to "be the change I wanted to see" in my profession related to the problems Black interpreters and those training to become interpreters faced on a regular basis. I asked myself, "Candas, what are YOU going to do about this?"

That question led me to declare that I am on a mission to literally change the face of ASL interpreting in the United

States by 2025. The most recent statistics, circa 2015, are that less than 5% of the interpreters in this country are Black, Latino, Asian, or from Indigenous populations. What this means is the large percentage of Deaf and hard-of-hearing people from these races and ethnicities rarely get to experience working with interpreters who look like them and/or share similar lived experiences. Therefore, they often need to code-switch from their natural way(s) of expressing themselves to accommodate the lack of cultural fluency many White interpreters have; this disfluency often results in miscommunication and misunderstandings.

My first step was to begin a movement by working with three colleagues to endow a scholarship fund at Gallaudet for students of color who want to become interpreters. That fund went from a concept in March of 2017 to a balance of nearly $54,000 as of this writing.

My next step? Answering the calling to teach interpreters that I had resisted for many years. A simple question from my coach, Alina Vincent, about why I wasn't doing something in my business to train interpreters as a way to leverage my decades of expertise and provide a service changed my entire life.

I've since come to claim my expertise as an educator, changemaker, inspiration, and business owner by founding the ASL Interpreting Academy and launching my first course, **ASL English Essentials**. This all happened when I said, "Yes."

For about 15 years prior to creating the course, I held a vision for a business that would give me time and financial freedom. I signed up for a plethora of programs and spent hundreds of thousands of dollars chasing the dream of becoming a successful entrepreneur only to repeatedly start, stall, sign up for another program, get excited, and stall again. While there was a part of me that believed I could succeed, after many years and a LOT of money, another part doubted.

Fortunately, in October 2020, I found myself face-to-face with the success I deeply desired but had been afraid of. I knew that creating courses for current and future interpreters could be wildly successful. Online interpreter training was an entrepreneur's dream—a focused and largely untapped niche. I had the expertise, the connections, the respect of colleagues and proteges, and the business training to make it work.

I only had to choose to make a difference for my waiting tribe!

I became highly sought after for my very specific expertise in watching Deaf people deliver messages in ASL and rendering clear and accurate spoken English interpretations. It is the primary skill that hinders or catapults interpreters' success, and I had mastered it, ensuring the Deaf consumers' voices were conveyed accurately so general audiences and, more specifically, their colleagues, friends, and family members who can hear understood them in ways that built bridges and dismantled barriers solely created by linguistic differences.

Despite the fact that colleagues and students begged me for years to teach, coach, or mentor them, I declined. I thought I was resisting because I didn't want to "only" be known for teaching interpreting. When I became painstakingly honest with myself, I was worried about being visible and responsible for getting it "right." I was worried that rather than seeking to support interpreters in doing a better job, I would be judged as trying to take advantage of the Deaf community. I was also afraid of what people would think of me for choosing to charge what this work and my expertise are worth. I was afraid of being as successful as I knew I could, and would, be. I questioned whether I had what it would take to successfully teach and make a difference. I doubted whether I knew how to best share what I had discovered and mastered, and whether I could create the infrastructure necessary to sustain a business *if* I managed to overcome all those other challenges.

Fortunately, when the student is ready, the teacher appears. Enter Alina. That question I mentioned she asked me opened my mind to an alternative to the fear I had let rule me. She gave me a different view of the possibility of my success by suggesting that I could create a course and potentially license it or train someone else to run it. This gave me just enough breathing room to get started.

My investment in Alina's Rising Stars Mastermind gave me a community of expert support that held me accountable and guided me toward achieving my dream of creating a successful business. This was a fortuitous thing, because after Alina sparked the vision, I could not get myself to tell anyone about the course I was thinking of creating.

Finally, one of the community coaches, Kristin, got me to test the waters by inviting me to post a simple offer on social media. After several days of procrastinating, I posted my progress on my Facebook profile and in a couple of groups for interpreters just five minutes before the deadline Kristin had given me. Before I knew it, people were reaching out to talk with me. I quickly lost count of how many.

Within a few days, I went from thinking about creating a course to enrolling 27 participants, generating $13,618, and having scores of people on a waiting list! About three weeks later, I launched my first cohort.

This proved that there's a hungry audience who needs what I have and who could decrease barriers, increase accessibility, and make a difference in the lives of any one of the over six million Deaf and hard-of-hearing people in the US alone.

Knowing this is my area of expertise, business owners often ask me about accessibility.

Here are some questions I often ask them:

- How many of your potential clients are Deaf? (Do you know?)

- Do you add captions to your videos?

- Do you provide transcripts for your video and audio content?

- When you have events, Zoom calls, gatherings of your tribe, etc., do you provide interpreters?

- Do you provide multiple ways of getting in touch with you if they want info about your products and services?

These simple questions provide awareness that opens doors previously shut. And if you'd like some tools and resources for making your own business more accessible, be sure to get a copy of my guide, 5 Tips for Making Your Business More Accessible, below.

By being willing to show up and make a difference, I've learned volumes about myself as a teacher and entrepreneur and about business development, running a course, growing a business, and taking care of my participants.

In four short months, I was able to serve 75 participants, generate $28,636, and donate over $5,000 to a number of endeavors related to the Deaf community, including the endowed scholarship fund at Gallaudet. None of that would have happened without my choosing to boldly move forward despite my internal objections and without leveraging my skills, talents, education, expertise, influence, connections, achievements, and successes.

I ran my first course, ASL English Essentials, in the midst of a *very* full personal and professional life that included a demanding full-time job at GIS, a part-time job in a huge technology retail company, and running a second business in the health and wellness industry. Additionally, we were in the midst of both the global COVID-19 pandemic and the worldwide civil rights crisis ignited by the murders of George Floyd and Breonna Taylor.

Both of these events set the stage for me to enroll participants who were hungry for what I had to offer into my trainings for working interpreters. They joined via Zoom from over 15 states and Puerto Rico, because they wanted to be better interpreters on behalf of the Deaf and hard-of-hearing people we serve and were ready to invest in themselves to do so.

Launching my online course allowed me to become more confident than I have ever been while doing my own work as an interpreter. I have an unwavering commitment to my own excellence and to promoting and encouraging excellence from my colleagues. The confidence I now have runs through my work in the Academy and in the work I do in my full-time position supervising staff interpreters in GIS—all a long way from where I started decades ago as a temp who didn't even know ASL.

As I think about leverage and what's possible through launching a course, I am aware that the impact the course has on others is important. For me, even more important is what Jim Rohn said: "The major reason for setting a goal is for what it makes of you to accomplish it. What it makes of you will always be the far greater value than what you get."

What I have gained from creating my course is invaluable. I've gotten clearer about what I do and how and why I do it. I've also learned how to talk about what I do in ways that support others in understanding how to effectively deliver spoken English messages on behalf of the Deaf and hard-of-hearing consumers they work with.

I love hearing from participants about their new discoveries related to the work and how they're coming to understand the importance of practicing the tools and techniques I've taught them. My heart swells when I hear from someone who has shifted from being complacent about his or her work to reinvigorated and more diligent in their daily practice.

Here's one of my favorite success stories:

Prior to taking ASL—English Essentials, one of my participants found herself unable to sleep soundly or to eat for days before going to an ASL-to-English assignment. Within less than three weeks after beginning the course, she was calm and confident before assignments and assertively seeking out opportunities for them. Since then, she has strengthened her capacity and expertise as an interpreter so much that she is considering interpreting opportunities she never would have even imagined herself doing a few months ago. In fact, she has now set her sights on fulfilling her lifelong dream of becoming a staff member with me at GIS, and I am delighted to be playing a part in her achieving that goal.

Creating this first online course is allowing me to leverage many things. When I began advertising it a second time, one of the senior members of our profession contacted me and donated payment for a full registration to the Academy's scholarship fund. Leveraging this connection and her influence opened the door for several participants to receive partial scholarships to courses and work on their craft.

Additionally, I leveraged my many years of experience in the field to help determine what my course participants needed to be successful. I used examples from my own success and from members of my sister circle to demonstrate concepts. I leveraged access I had to materials to provide participants with a library of content to practice the techniques and skills they were seeking to master.

I learned that working with a group allows me to leverage the power of cohort learning—which is ultimately so much more effective and efficient than working one-on-one. I created a community of practice where the participants feel comfortable working together and are willing to be vulnerable while reviewing and examining their work with one another—unusual, for professionals in our field. They now have a camaraderie and regularly network. These are people whose paths may never have crossed if not for my course. Now, they are committed to doing their best work and supporting one another along the way. All because I let my mission be my driving force!

Plus, they can and do learn from one another, sometimes even more so than through working with me as the "leader." By having participants share about their wins and takeaways, others were able to recognize and share their own. Also, when participants saw someone else having success, they became more inclined to take risks to increase their own chances of "winning."

To illustrate this point, just two days after the "meet and greet" for the second cohort of my course, one of the participants shared this online:

"So since we are in a voicing workshop, I wanted to share that I just had an assignment that required a lot of voicing. I have always said that is not my strong suit... well, that ends today. I rocked my voicing portion. I kept all of you, especially Candas, in my head the entire time. I'm so proud of myself, and although we haven't done much work yet, I credit this group."

She felt confident in her work and knew she had a community that supported and encouraged her. As much as what I teach matters, leaning into the power of the community exponentially increased her self-confidence and empowered her to do work she wasn't as confident about just a few days before.

Something else that is now crystal clear to me is that there are people who are waiting for us course creators to do the thing we know we have to do.

Dear reader, you already have an expertise that someone is looking for. We often believe we have to have it all together before we can support someone else. The truth is, we only have to offer what we already have, and it gets magnified and multiplied in ways we can't begin to foresee.

As you think about how to leverage your knowledge, skills, abilities, and connections into your own business, consider taking these steps:

1. Study: What are the basics of your craft?

2. Find role models: Who is successfully doing what you're seeking to do? Who do you admire?

3. Prepare: What do you need to know about your craft that can support you in being successful? What do your role models do to prepare that you can learn from?

4. Practice: How can you find/create opportunities to practice?

5. Catch yourself (and others) doing good: What are you doing that's working? What can you do more of that you're already doing?

The biggest thing I wish I'd known before creating an online course is how important it is to "just do it." Get started. Pick a date and launch—no matter what. Figure it out as you're in it.

Make a difference: your tribe is waiting!

***

Candas Ifama Barnes is a pioneering African American linguistic alchemist. She uses written and spoken words to create change, build connections, and foster community. She is Founder and CEO of The ASL Interpreting Academy, a comprehensive, multifaceted training institute for American Sign Language (ASL) interpreters and those who want to become interpreters. Candas' career as an ASL - English interpreter focuses on producing bond-building spoken English messages from ASL source texts. In 2016, she coined the term "culturally-responsive interpreting" to describe the phenomenon that occurs when Deaf people work with interpreters who are culturally equipped to effectively convey their messages. By 2025, she is committed to exponentially increasing the number of Black and Brown ASL interpreters from less than 5% to more than 20%. Responding to the escalating demand for well-trained, culturally fluent "voice" interpreters, Candas founded the Academy in October 2020.

LeverageYourExpertiseBook.com/gifts

Get Candas's free gift ...

5 Tips for Making Your Business More Accessible to open your business and services up to 6,000,000 new leads and customers, here:

LeverageYourExpertiseBook.com/gifts

Leverage Your Expertise

Chapter 7
Showing Up for YOU
by Erin Arnold

As I glanced at the incoming photo text on my phone, I saw my daughter's smiling face at her class party.

And I burst into tears.

I wasn't able to be there. Again.

I had gone to physical therapy school 15 years before with idealistic dreams of being able to help every person who walked through my door for physical therapy.

And while I *had* been able to help thousands of people who were in various degrees of discomfort and suffering with issues like bladder leakage, painful intercourse, and pelvic pain, I realized my professional life and ability to practice my craft were being dictated by insurance limitations, documentation requirements, and my boss's own bottom line.

I had no freedom to be able to take time off for my daughter's school holidays, let alone her classroom parties. And I was spending hours of my own time after work finishing my treatment notes every single night. It wasn't how I wanted to show up for my family, or myself.

So, I made a plan that day to start my own physical therapy clinic and private practice, and Central Texas Myofascial Release was born about a year later.

Finally, I was seeing patients on a schedule that worked for me and my family! I had also created my business model in a way that would allow me to work for patients instead of insurance companies, which I loved.

My practice grew and grew. I typically had at least a three-month wait time before someone was able to get in to see me. And for five wonderful years, it was fantastic. I finally had the work-life balance I craved and the freedom to treat my patients the way they deserved to be treated!

But then… March 2020 happened.

Much like the rest of the world, my practice ground to a halt as I made the decision to temporarily close my clinic while the world tried to figure out what we collectively needed to do to try and slow the spread of COVID-19.

And for the first time since my teenage years, I actually had a break from nearly constant work. It takes an immense amount of time and training to become a physical therapist, and almost that same amount of time and effort to continue to improve your skills.

And there I was, in March and April of 2020, with time to enjoy my previously neglected backyard swing, watch the spring flowers bloom, and once again re-evaluate where I was in relation to where I wanted to go with my life.

I realized that as much as I loved what I did, the practice I created, and the people I was helping, I would always be trading time for money. And as my waiting list demonstrated, there was never going to be enough of me to go around to be able to help all the people I wanted to when and if I was able to return to seeing patients in person again.

You see, my physical therapy specialty, pelvic floor physical therapy, is still not very well-known, and there are not many physical therapists who specialize in it.

Many people don't know that bladder leakage is never normal, that having sex without pain is possible, that constipation can cause a myriad of pelvic issues, that pain in and around their genitals doesn't have to be there forever, or that there are people like me who can help with all of that and more.

For years, I had thought about creating online courses to help train younger pelvic floor physical therapists, but I never had the time to devote to it.

But with my "Covid Break" and a lot of self-reflection, I realized creating programs for other therapists wasn't going to nourish my soul and align with my purpose. Instead, I wanted to create programs for *regular* people. I wanted to reach those who didn't have access to a pelvic health physical therapist like me due to location, time, or resources. What I didn't know, however, was the first thing about creating, marketing, and leveraging an online course. Truly, I was clueless about the online world.

At that pivotal moment, I was introduced to Alina Vincent.

She helped me focus on one idea, create a framework for program creation, and have the confidence to step into this online world. I dutifully followed her step-by-step system for developing an online course.

Within two months of meeting Alina, I had created a new company, Weaving Wellness, to be the online arm of my business. I had 15 people from five different states enrolled in my pilot program, **Bladder Boss,** and I had also gone back to treating patients in person full-time in my clinic.

In hindsight, I am glad I came into Alina's program a little clueless. If I had realized the amount of time and effort it takes to launch a successful, sustainable online business, I'm not sure I would have said "Yes!" If I'm honest, I still sometimes wonder about saying it.

But I also realize that what I am creating has the potential to leverage my 20 years of therapy expertise to help people in many places—even internationally. And it has already begun.

I have not only been able to offer my online course to people all over the world, but I have also leveraged my time and my knowledge by offering the Bladder Boss course to clients on my waiting list.

When clients come to my clinic with bladder issues, I often spend those early visits on exactly the kind of education I provide in my online course. For less complex clinical cases, this education might be all some need to implement to get to where they want to be. For more complicated cases, more hands-on treatment and modifications may be necessary. In either case, it might be a better use of my clients' time and resources to utilize the online course training and limit the number of visits they might need to have with me or another physical therapist in person, if at all!

While I created Bladder Boss with an eye toward leveraging my time and experience, my intention has always been to get quality, vetted information about pelvic health to women.

I have been overwhelmed with the positive response I had from the participants of the course. Well over 90% of respondents have had a decrease in their bladder leakage as a result of taking it!

Many of the women who have taken Bladder Boss have been suffering from bladder leakage for years and just did not know what to do or where to go for help. They had resolved themselves to the fact that their issues were never going to change.

Sandy, a 57-year-old retired teacher, is a perfect example. Now a grandmother and caretaker of a young grandson, she was noticing more and more that her bladder was ruling her life. She was scared it would leak every time she lifted her grandson out of his crib, or when she was chasing him around the house, or even when she was out and about shopping. She had brought up her issues to her doctor, but was blown off after being told it was just something that "happened to women her age."

During the course, we met weekly for group discussion about how the course was going. Around week three, I could tell there was something—an energy—building inside her, but she wasn't ready to share. I circled back to her at the end of the hour and asked her if there was anything she would like to bring to the group.

Her jaw set. Her face and chest began to flush. She paused, collecting her thoughts. As a group, we sat in that silent space with her, supporting her. After a few minutes, she gathered herself, jaw still bulging, and yelled, "I'M SO MAD!!!" I stopped in my tracks. Was she mad at the course? Mad at me? I centered myself and waited.

She continued: "I'm so MAD that I have had this issue for YEARS, and I have brought this to my doctor, and asked my friends, and no one has ever done anything to help me. I have been doing this online course for only three weeks, and the things you are teaching AREN'T EVEN HARD TO DO, and almost all my symptoms are gone. Why hasn't anyone taught me this before?!"

The other women in the group started nodding their heads in agreement. Knowing they weren't alone in their bladder issues and that there was something they could do was life-changing for them.

And the change was happening from an online course. The one I had created.

Maybe you can relate to Sandy. Maybe you have been privately having occasional (or not-so-occasional) bladder leakage. Maybe you hope it will just go away on its own, because you are not sure what to do otherwise.

If so, I have some great beginner tips for you!

3 Tips to Start Your Journey Back to Bladder Control

1. Fill out a Bladder Diary.

Many women are familiar with the concept of completing a food diary if they are trying to lose weight or to identify a food that might be causing them symptom upset.

A bladder diary works in a similar way.

When we track what we are drinking, when we are drinking it, when we are urinating, and when we might be having leakage, we can start to spot trends and patterns.

Once those patterns are identified, it is so much easier to make simple behavioral adjustments which are easy to integrate but have the potential to make huge changes in regard to bladder leakage.

2. Next, take a break from doing Kegel exercises.

Did I just blow your mind?

While most people think that doing Kegel (pelvic floor muscle) exercises will solve their bladder issues, it can actually make the problem worse. What happens is that the clenching puts those muscles in a shortened position, which makes them less able to respond when coughing, sneezing, laughing, or having a sudden urge to pee.

If we wanted to strengthen our bicep muscle, we wouldn't run around all day with our elbow fully bent and our wrist by our shoulders, would we? That would be silly! It's the exact same with the muscles of our pelvic floor.

Kegels certainly have their place in pelvic floor rehab. But if you have been doing Kegels round-the-clock without improvement, it might be a sign that it isn't the best option for where your body is now.

3. Swap out those Kegels for something better!

Wait, there are better exercises for the pelvic floor heath than Kegels?

Yep!

Your local pelvic floor physical therapist is almost always the best person to assess your body and give you the most targeted suggestions for your own body.

But there are some common things you can try that will not ever harm you.

Often times, these exercises can feel deceptively simple. But it is in their simplicity, portability, and ease that makes them all the more productive and successful.

If you would like my suggestion for the one exercise for the pelvic floor that is better than Kegels, I hope you check out my free gift below!

Give these tips a try—I'm confident you'll start to feel a difference in your bladder symptoms, pelvic pain, and dare I add—possibly *even your orgasms!* Practicing self-care, for your bladder and for the rest of your body, cultivating joy, and continuing to nurture your relationships are essential to both your personal and professional success.

Now, I realize you might not have picked up this book because you are passionate about learning about bladder leakage from a physical therapist, although I do hope you learned something. If you did, I also hope you "pay it forward" by sharing it with other women in your life.

Instead, you are most likely here to learn how other entrepreneurs went about leveraging their expertise with an online program and how you can do the same.

We all have gifts and expertise that the world needs us to share. Creating and leveraging online courses around your passion is the perfect vehicle for doing so. And since you are here, you have most likely heard that call to share your gifts.

Throughout this book, I hope you have found some inspiring stories and actionable advice. To that end, following is my own advice based on hard-earned lessons I learned along the way. I hope they'll help guide you through the course-creation process as you leverage your expertise:

1. Know that this process is a marathon, not a sprint.
   Building and marketing a successful online business is something that takes time, consistency, and persistence. While you need to work intentionally on your business and growing your audience, it should *not* be something that overtakes every minute of your life. Make sure to make time for you, your relationships, and your health during the process.

2. Not everything you try will work.
   Things often work out differently than how we thought they would. Every option you try will give you the opportunity to assess, modify, and improve your message to your ideal clients.

3. Hire a coach
   We need people who care about us, but who can also see our business through another set of eyes. Having skilled outside feedback is vital to understanding our own limiting beliefs and self-imposed barriers to success and in helping us grow.

4. Stay true to yourself and your own voice.
   While coaches and colleagues are helpful with needed advice, remember that in the end, your business is yours. No one has your voice and your message. Be coachable, but always come back to trusting your own voice and intuition.

I wish you the success you deserve, and I can't wait to see what you create!

***

Erin Arnold, PT, MPT, LMT is a passionate advocate for her patients and for pelvic health. Her background in John F Barnes Myofascial Release has allowed her to see bodies as whole and dynamic systems, which has strongly influenced her treatment of pelvic floor conditions. Her mission is to arm her clients with the confidence and awareness to trust their own bodies, their signals, and their ability to heal. Her online courses combine her decades of clinical practice, love of education, and deep desire to help others move toward the highest expression of their lives. You can learn more about her here: weavingwellness.com.

Get Erin's free gift …

The One Exercise That Is Better For Your Pelvic Floor Than Kegels to start on your journey to less bladder leakage, decreased pelvic pain, and better orgasms, here:

LeverageYourExpertiseBook.com/gifts

Leverage Your Expertise

Chapter 8
It Only Takes One to Start the Change
by Aneta Chencinski

My arrival at the door of my career as a parenting coach was driven by personal need.

My daughter was a happy, obedient, and easy-to-parent child, so I was totally unprepared to deal with my second strong-minded child. A gorgeous red-haired son with character to match, he would listen to what I said with intense concentration, and then shrug his shoulders and do whatever he wanted. I fast realized I had no tools to effectively deal with his will, and that I needed help… I needed to learn how to parent him the right way.

Six years later, after attending three hours of WEEKLY classes totaling 900+ hours, I was still going strong. I learned, I assisted, and I coached.

The first months of my journey into a "new parenting land" were difficult and painful. I had to disregard and often turn upside down my parenting-related thoughts and actions. But after a fair share of crying, rebelling, and even cursing, I started to incorporate the techniques I learned into our family life. My husband also started to apply those methods, *and change happened!*

The puzzle rearranged itself, and life become more joyful and less chaotic. Halleluiah!

Our kids grew into marvellous human beings. Loving, independent, generous adults. We often hear, *"You've raised a good one"* from friends, neighbors, and co-workers. And I agree—we have, and we were very lucky! We did a great job with the help of the Adler Parenting School program.

I know firsthand that it is possible for parents and kids to enjoy the adolescent years and have respectful and loving interactions throughout that turbulent period. Parents can have a close connection with their kids, and kids can continue to enjoy freedom, respect, and a great relationship with their siblings and parents.

That is why I chose to be a parenting coach. Contributing to individual and family happiness gives meaning to my life.

Through my business, Happy Family by Design, grownups learn a new approach to parenting and get the support they need, so their families can benefit as greatly as mine has. It is a win-win situation.

Working with individuals face to face (or Zoom to Zoom, now) is very fulfilling; however, I realized I don't have enough time to make the impact I wanted to by supporting as many families as possible. I was looking for leverage solutions, and I found one with Alina Vincent's help—creating an online program.

Creating my online program, **The Parent-Teen Connection**, allows me to reach multiple families at the same time anywhere at the world. And that means Happy Families by Design can reach more people, create more positive impact, and help transform the lives of more families than ever before!

Allow me to quote my clients:

"Our meetings are extremely helpful in coaching us to respond properly to their [adolescents'] *behavior, to set goals, and to slowly get toward them. While we are in the beginning only, we see improvement in some of the aspects and in the way our parenting functions."*

"Aneta is clearly experienced with children and marital challenges. She was instrumental in helping guide me as a new parent to be more patient, caring, and connected to my child and spouse during difficult times"

"Aneta keeps me to my word. I would take up her time every day if I could."

Creating an online program was not easy. It forced me to confront my fears, make myself visible in a way I never have before, and discover many limiting beliefs I did not even know were hiding inside me.

Day after day, I had to battle with new uncertainties, new fears, and new obstacles. Transferring the knowledge from my head to the paper and organizing and ordering the content was overwhelming, because I wasn't sure how to do it in a coherent way. I also had fears around not being able to deliver.

However, there were only two choices—sink or swim! Wrestle with the insecurities and overcome them, or decide to abandon the program and go back to where I was before I joined Alina's Rising Stars Mastermind.

Lucky for me, RSM offers a lot of support and coaching. With energy, emotional, and marketing support from copywriting coaches and personalized guidance as well as support from fellow participants, I was able to overcome my fears and create and deliver the pilot version of my program! And what an amazing realization came with that accomplishment...

I can do it!

This process helped me grow and evolve. I am a different person now—more capable, trusting of myself, self-assured, and ready for challenges life will bring (because it always does). I learned to ask for help, to be vulnerable, to show my fears and uncertainties, and to trust myself and others.

My other huge win? The woman who looks back at me in the mirror is stronger, braver, and more self-assured and assertive. I like her more now!

I also now have time… to enjoy evenings with my family and friends, for my hobbies, and to travel. I have the freedom to decide where, when, and how to spend my time and money.

All while helping parents establish stronger relationships with their kids, which I love to do!

In fact, if you are a parent, you might want to try the following simple-but-powerful exercise. It's designed to help all the members of your family learn more about the impact each person has on the family unit as whole. Because the simple truth is that we all matter, and we are all important. Never underestimate the power of influence one person has on family life. You can, singlehandedly, change the interactions in your family.

Exercise: Family Connections

Step 1: Grab a piece of string about six-to-seven feet long (around 200 cm). Tie the ends together, so you have a closed loop.

Step 2: From additional string, cut a new 1.5-foot-string for each family member. (If you have four people in your family, cut four pieces.)

Step 3: At equal intervals, tie each 1.5-foot-string to the six-foot-string loop.

Step 4: Next, each member takes in hand the loose end of a short string. Take two steps backward, so the long string forms a loop.

Step 5. Ask the youngest member of the family to take one step backward without releasing the string while maintaining the shape.

By stepping back, the string in the youngest person's hand will gently pull on one side, causing the other family members to take a small step forward or to the side. All the family members will be affected by the movement and have to move in response.

Step 6: Reiterate the lesson: When one person in the family changes or does something, all the family members are influenced. Every person matters; every person is important; every person creates an impact.

I love this exercise, and so do my clients. If you are a parent looking for ways to connect with your children and show them how influential and important they are, I hope you will give it a try.

And if you are an entrepreneur with a message to share, here is what I want to leave you with:

1. Don't hide!

Show the world what you have to offer and who you are! You have the expertise you need, and if you are looking for ways to share it with the world to leverage your impact, RSM is the right place for you. If you doubt you have what it takes, I can assure you that, with the right support and in the right environment, you can deliver your message to the world. You will find strength to overcome your fears, and in the process, you will also grow as a person. How can I be sure? Because I did it. And that means it's possible for you, too.

2. Learn how to deliver your message by creating an online program. When you do, you'll impact more people than you can imagine.

3. Leverage your time and money by creating an online program. You will have more time to do things you love.

My biggest lesson learned on the online course-creation journey? **Don't do it by yourself.** If I continued working by myself, I would not have been in the place I am today.

Having a mentor, supportive community, and place where I could ask questions and feel safe were essential to my journey. I am so grateful I found RSM and decided to invest in myself. Yes, it is work; yes, it takes time. But what bliss is on the other side!

I hope you are ready for your journey!

***

Aneta Chencinski is a registered Psychotherapist, Life Coach, and counselor specializing in working with parents of adolescents and ADHD-affected teens. She has more than 20 years of experience supporting individuals and families on their journey to happier, more fulfilling lives and satisfying relationships. You can learn more about her here: www.therapywithaneta.com.

Get Aneta's free gift …

Stop Arguing with Your Kids: 3 Golden Rules That Will Keep Your Household Quiet and Peaceful to improve your relationship with your teenager, here:

LeverageYourExpertiseBook.com/gifts

Leverage Your Expertise

Chapter 9
Awaken Your Authentic Voice
by Diann Alexander

Do you ever feel there is something deep inside you that you know you're meant to share, but it doesn't seem to ever come out on stage the way you imagine it in your head? Perhaps you have a looming fear that no one will like it… or worse, like you! Maybe you think if you don't do a good job, you will disappoint others and embarrass yourself. You won't be able to perform on stage or screen the way you did in practice.

How can you get it out of your mouth and onto the stage or screen with confidence, clarity, and audience connection? How can you grow to truly shine on stage or screen?

If this sounds familiar, I'm so glad you're reading this!

Your voice matters. You matter. Your gifts matter.

And awakening your authentic voice may be one of the most powerful, rewarding, and contributive experiences you ever have. It was for me.

Beginnings

Growing up, there was a great deal of conflict in my home. My M.O. was to either be the peacemaker or make myself small and hide.

Much of my life was spent in "freeze" mode. Don't inflame. Be very quiet. Hide. If I followed all the rules, I would be okay. Things would turn my way at some point, right?

So, in school, I strove to be the absolute best student. Later, I did the same in my roles as composer, performer, daughter, and wife. These are the external identities we wear that we think are really us and therefore define us.

But at 33, everything changed. I packed up my belongings on a Tuesday, got divorced on a Wednesday, and drove away that Thursday in a 12-foot U-Haul, towing my car and three prized possessions: my waterbed, my Everett piano, and my beloved Sheltie Mix, Jenny. As I drove from Michigan to California, I felt I didn't belong anywhere. It was astounding, odd, and freeing all at the same time.

Who was I, when not attached to all those identities?

In California, all of the identities that used to define me no longer existed. Without the structures of home, education, family, and teaching, finding a new identity was definitely an unexpected E-ticket ride.

That familiar need to be the perfect everything was still very real at this point, and when nothing came through, I fell into despair. One night, my head hurt so badly, I actually banged it on the floor trying to get the pain to stop. It was agony. It seemed everything I had been told about being perfect and having a good life was a story, a lie, and I was completely lost.

Having no one around to advise me, I slowly began to realize **that I was the one who had to choose what was important to me—I had to choose not to hide.**

It seemed nearly blasphemous! However, with no other options, I chose to start with being loving, kind, and honest with myself about how I was feeling no matter what. There would be no more glossing over, ignoring, burying, or making myself small so others would feel comfortable.

Over the next few decades, I watched the effects of the awakening of my voice… of being my honest, true, playful, interactive, loving, uplifted self had on others. I became so much more effective in my communications than when I was trying to keep myself small.

Being Versus Doing

The next chapter of my life became about *being* versus doing. Who was I really, now that I was in charge of each step of my life?

I have always been a teacher—from being the "Game Fairy" at birthday parties when I was ten to this day, nearly 60 years later, having been a vocal instructor and founder of Healthy Singing Voice Studio, Sound Bath Serenity, and Sound Energy Flow. My life has always been about giving audiences an inclusive, uplifting, and memorable experience. Of course, I didn't know that at the time. What I knew was connecting with people, whether through game, story, song, or play. It was completely rewarding.

It is still my passion, as it still fascinates me after all these years. When the pieces fit together and a student "gets it" and delivers what is in their hearts to the best of their ability, I still get tears. It is a profound and underrated occurrence.

As the teacher, I know the more I am myself, the more clearly I see my students and can create a loving, safe, and playful vibration, so they feel safe to explore who they really are.

And I have always been driven to empower my students, colleagues, friends, and acquaintances to see the best in themselves and connect them with their inner singer presenter.

My Personal Passion

Now, my personal passion is to share my combined 50 years teaching voice, theatre, and performance techniques in universities, professional groups, and privately with my 25 years as an energy facilitator with the magic of Alchemy Crystal Singing Bowls to create a unique journey inward for my clients—to bring their true, authentic self out into the light! This way, they can make real connections and a lasting impact while moving their audience.

Because in my experience, what truly makes a presenter stand out is not the outer mechanics—not just how he or she moves, walks, talks, and looks on stage (although those things help, none alone will capture your audience). It's their own connection to their inner knowing, their authentic true self, and their special message. Because the audience wants the real you… the sparkle and the vulnerability, together.

Why is that harder to provide than one might think?

Well, the truth is, we tend to lose touch with our inner purpose. Think about it: in school, we are so busy following our teachers' instructions, we often let go of our own experience and give our power and approval to those outside of us. That inner purpose remains, nudging us, but the outer world hits us with so many restrictions and rules that we lose our nerve. We may even lose touch with our special message altogether.

Think of what attracts you to a presenter. What pulls you in, captivates you, connects with you? What is that special quality that makes him or her stand out from others? What touches your heart and catches your fancy? What makes you remember a presenter long after the event?

Presentations with perfect technical mastery but with no heart or emotional connection fall flat. I have also witnessed presentations in which the presenter was not technically perfect, yet was completely present, vulnerable, and accessible, sharing her true inner essence. *These* are the presentations and performances we tend to remember long after they end and share with our friends. Audiences long for that real connection.

When people connect with their true inner knowing and share their vulnerable, honest self, the stage is theirs. Communication, whether in the spotlight, on the screen, or in person, blossoms. True connection is made. When you uplift, intrigue, edify, entertain, or engage even one person in your audience, you have made a difference in a life, and your presentation is a success. He or she will take and share that experience, uplifting others, and the inspiration continues to ripple out into the world. It can do so much good!

And that is what I teach my students.

The Pivot

Then, COVID-19 hit. Before the pandemic, I had no thought of creating an online program. I was happily and successfully teaching privately. Word-of-mouth was my only marketing, and things were going well.

However, afterward, teaching private voice online became an entirely different endeavor. The myriad technical problems—from sound lag, difficulties hearing the full spectrum of sound, not being to sing with or hear the student simultaneously—diminished my ability to personally guide or demonstrate for students with either voice or piano. There were so many technical challenges to solve that it took so much joy out of the process. Plus, the wonderfully close, personalized learning experience I prided myself on was now forced into long distance. My teaching was handicapped, and I knew I had to find another way.

Creating an online program seemed the most logical, leveraged way to continue being of service without having to work one-on-one for every dollar. So, I began taking online business and course-creation classes, looking to find a business mentor who "got me"—one who would narrow everything down and help me focus my "Ooo shiny!" nature by providing me with a step-by-step plan. After about six months, I found Alina. I was hooked when she stated, "You do the content; I do the structure."

She was clear, and I could understand her. She was also a walking model of what I wanted to accomplish.

Imagine my surprise when the first instruction was "Sell it before you write it." WHAT? I come from a long line of educators, composers, and writers. With musical productions, every detail must be organized before you sell tickets. This seemed wrong and completely counterintuitive to everything I'd learned in my university training and teaching. I struggled; how could I take advice from someone who doesn't even know the subject?

However, I conceded. Alina is wildly successful, which is largely why I chose her as a mentor. So, I held my breath, created an outline for a foundational course, and embarked on my course-creation journey.

Following Alina's advice to choose ONE angle only, I ultimately decided I could make the strongest impact by dealing with a problem almost all of my clients—and 75% of the population, according to the National Institute of Mental Health—come up against at some point or another: stage fright.

Yes! I would combine my lifetime of teaching and performance experience with sound and energy to compile a series of practical, useful, immediately applicable exercises that would allow others to share their authentic gifts with confidence!

Creating and running the pilot, the first maiden voyage of my Awaken the Singer Within course, was illuminating. I earned nearly $1,000 in sales at a low entry price.

In addition, Alina brought new light to the word "leverage." In the Rising Stars Mastermind, I had access to an entire group of like-minded entrepreneurs who were on the exact same path I was in regard to leveraging their businesses. We were able to exchange ideas, receiving and providing feedback. This community leveraged our time as we brainstormed and shared suggestions and experiences. Together, we were much more effective.

One of the biggest benefits of creating the online program in terms of leverage has been learning about joint venture partners. With a "How can I help you?" perspective, JV partners meet and "pitch" their projects to find similar and complementary partners to share and exchange marketing ventures. My world exploded with possibilities! Attending only three networking virtual events, I now have numerous invitations to appear on podcasts, been a featured presenter in a summit, recorded a television interview, been invited to teach a module in another highly accomplished JV's course, *and* participated in several Giveaways. I feel like I found the pot of gold!

These successful JV marketing strategies leverage my professional expertise and my partners' marketing experience. Together, we create a long-term, mutually supportive relationship that can support both our businesses in growing exponentially. Competition has been replaced with collaboration, and it is so inspiring!

From Nervous to Noteworthy

My students love the online format, as well. While I distinctly remember wishing there were more hours in the day while creating the course, the feedback I received from people like Quinn truly helped me tailor the content into an even more user-friendly format:

Quinn was a professional counselor and presenter. She was also a long-time competitive Sweet Adeline Singer who, despite years of experience and competitions, could barely walk on stage without shaking, sweating, struggling with her breath. During the final week of the course, she was able to put her training into practice and make a solid, confident entrance and delight her audience with her presentation! She transformed right before our eyes. Other members of that class remember her brave and dramatic transformation to this day. After years of debilitating stage fright, she experienced success!

Honestly, nothing makes me happier than stories like Quinn's.

Which is why I also want to share an exercise with you today to help you calm yourself down before getting on stage, if you happen to be one of the 75% of people who fear public speaking.

Understanding the fight, flight, or freeze response is crucial to developing confidence-building practices. It is the reflex all living beings experience when they feel threatened. The breath shuts down, the chest caves, and the back of the neck contracts. All energy is diverted to extremities, so you can fight, flee, or freeze in response to the perceived danger. It is hard to think when this response is active, let alone to remember your words or connect with your audience.

Calming breathing techniques can become your best friends when you're combatting fear. Breathing shallowly can trigger the strangling FFF response, while breathing into the lower lungs and allowing your belly to stretch down and open produces a calming response.

Exercise: The Central Channel Breath (From Dr. Sue Morter's Energy Codes®)

Step 1: Envision an open, lit pathway running from overhead down through the center of your body, then down your legs and out your feet. This is the Central Channel.

Step 2: Place your hands on your lower belly. Thumbs toward the navel, clasp your fingers together as low as you are able.

Step 3. Inhale deeply and s-l-o-w-l-y through your nose. Feel your breath fill your low belly, low and around, much like a water balloon. The water goes into the bottom, then around to the sides. Hold it a few seconds, and let it feel good.

Step 4: As you exhale, use your hands to bring your lower abdomen in and up while s-l-o-w-l-y breathing out through your nose.

Step 5: Imagine the next inhale coming up from the center of the Earth, through your legs, and stretching out your lower belly in all directions. Hold it a few seconds. Let it feel good.

Step 6: Bring the belly button back to the spine as you exhale up and out through the solar plexus, heart, throat, middle of the brain, and out the top of the head.

Step 7: Reverse the flow. Imagine the air coming in from overhead, flowing through the brain, throat, heart, and solar plexus into the belly—your wisdom center. Hold it a few seconds, and let it feel good.

Step 8: Keeping your chest up and open, exhale the air all the way down through the legs and back into Mother Earth.

Complete three to ten rounds of this breath every time you think of it. By doing so, you are building calming, confident neurological circuitry. The more often you can practice, the quicker your results!

There are many pieces to running an online business and creating an online program. My advice is, if you are new to the tech side, allow extra time to get set up right. It's also a smart idea to hire a mentor or virtual assistant.

If you are inspired to go this route, follow your heart, trust your gut, and share your message, get started now!

***

Diann Alexander, BS, MM, MM, Energy Codes® Certified Master Trainer, empowers speakers, presenters, and singers to deliver their heartfelt message with confidence and authenticity. Her special sauce is combining three advanced degrees, 50 years of voice teaching and music directing, 35 years of energy facilitation and the magic of Alchemy Crystal Singing Bowls to help Presenters uncover their authenticity and confidently bring it to the stage. Your onstage radiance will indeed grow your confidence, clarity, and connection. From Stage Fright to Stage Might, she awakens your authentic voice. You can learn more about her here: https://diannalexander.com.

Get Diann's free gift …

5 Offstage Keys to Onstage Radiance to dial in on the details of unlocking your unique message in an authentic, confident, and clear presentation that engages your audiences and inspires them to buy and tell their friends here:

LeverageYourExpertiseBook.com/gifts

Chapter 10
Find Your Divine Path and Live Your Purpose
by Carmen Gélinas MBA

I always felt that I belonged in nature; wherever I can listen to the world, see the little animals flitting by, and hear the birds chirping, I feel like myself. I feel at once free and connected to the Divine.

But often, it's during times of turmoil that we most need to access that connection. Because when we're in transition or experiencing heartache, we may feel uncertain about what's "right" in the moment.

What I've come to realize is…

When we access our connection with the Divine, we can have the peace we crave.

This is what I am called to teach others: to connect with their Divine Wisdom to find their true paths. What makes me happy is that I'm now able to reach people around the world with my message… while walking my own path with certainty and peace of mind.

You see, as an adult, I had several Divine experiences—situations in which I felt like I was receiving guidance or reassurance from my Divine Wisdom. It brought me such a sense of certainty that I knew I had to help other people reconnect with their Divine Wisdom. I knew that by doing so, I could guide people in changing their lives.

Born and raised in Evain, a small village near the city of Rouyn-Noranda in Northern Quebec, Canada, I come from a family of seven children. Like many in my family and community, we had adult responsibilities beginning at a young age. I started working when I was 10 years old—I spent my afternoons and evenings after school and my summers putting in time at our family-owned print shop, garage, and taxi dispatch. At 18, I moved on to work for others in a hardware store, and then, a propane store.

At 19, I moved away to Ottawa, Ontario, Canada, where I am now, and started a job with the federal government as a typist. I got married at 20, had my daughter at 22, and divorced my husband at 27. A newly single mom, I couldn't afford to pay off all the debt I'd racked up, so at 28, I declared bankruptcy and lost everything, including my house.

I had to start from zero. My daughter and I moved into an apartment, and I soon started dating again. During one relationship that lasted several years, my partner constantly psychologically abused me. I contemplated suicide many times, but knew my daughter needed me.

When I finally gathered the courage to leave him, he didn't take it well.

He broke into my apartment in the middle of the night and kidnapped me at gunpoint. He drove me to a new place he'd rented.

Needless to say, I was terrified. I'd never been that scared in my life.

Inside his apartment, I sat down at the table, and he just stood there, staring at me, the gun in his hand. I didn't know what to do or say—other than to pray to God that if something happened to me, my daughter would be safe. It felt like hours passed, and I prayed and prayed.

And then at one point, I felt a huge current of energy run through my body, from head to toe. I had the utmost feeling, the certainty, that everything was going to be alright.

I was—and am—100% certain that it was a Divine Intervention… an answer to my prayers.

With a new sense of calm, I got up and asked him what he wanted. He told me that he wanted to be with me one last time. I allowed him even though I was numb and did not feel anything the whole entire time. The only thing I kept thinking is that everything was going to be alright… that the Divine was going to be there for me from now on. When he was done, he let me go.

I spent the next seven years as a single mom, and I dove deep into personal and spiritual development. I read hundreds of books, listened to hundreds of recordings, and attended seminars, classes, online courses, and more. I took in every piece of information I could from all the greats: Neal Donald Walsh, Oprah Winfrey, Wayne Dyer, Eckhart Tolle, Esther Hicks, Jane Robert, Godfré Ray King, Doreen Virtue, David R. Hawkins, Lise Bourbeau, Vianna Stibal, and many more.

After making progress in my job, which was then in information technology, I bought a new house, and my daughter and I moved in. I was proud of myself. I had climbed out of the despair of a traumatic relationship and bankruptcy and was determined to succeed. I felt at peace with myself and was set on building my understanding and relationship with the Divine. And while I was happy as a single mom, I had a new divine purpose, and I was lucky enough for the Universe to send me a wonderful man who became my husband in 2004.

When my baby sister, my closest family member, died from cancer in 2005 at the age of 40, leaving behind two young kids, it rocked me to my core. I was there when she took her last breath, and it was the most serene experience I have ever had knowing that she was at peace as she transitioned into her new chapter with the Divine.

My faith in the Divine and my experiences helped me through it, and although I did not have all the tools, understanding, and knowledge I have today, it gave me even more conviction that my path was correct.

Finally, I felt at peace within myself.

Around this same time, my daughter and I created a personal life coaching business, Let's Talk… Coaching & Energy Healing. Three years later, in 2014, I retired from government after over thirty years of service. The coaching business took off, and since then, my life has changed profoundly for the better; being a spiritual teacher and energy healer is the most wonderful thing I have done.

And while I coached others, I continued my own learning, as well. I devoured absolutely everything I could about spirituality, energy healing, and coaching, and the process transformed my life.

The biggest impact the energy healing had on me is that it helped me rebuild my relationship with my father. We'd never had a close relationship; I never took the time to have a meaningful conversation with him, because I never felt like he understood where I was coming from. But after learning a powerful energy healing technique, I used it on myself and was then able to go back to the source of the problems between my father and me and repair them with what the Divine told me was for my highest and best good.

Not too long after that, I went to my parents' house, sat at the table with my father, and had the best conversation with him I'd ever had in my life.

I was amazed at the power of energy healing.

As I've continued to have experiences with the Divine—healing, enlightening, life-changing experiences—I realized that I needed to share this knowledge and these experiences with others. Providing energy healing sessions and seminars gives me a front-row seat to the positive changes that occur in my clients' attitude, personal growth, and confidence, and it is heartwarming and incredibly satisfying.

Eventually, though I had created a successful business around proven energy healing techniques, I began searching for more ways to reach people. I knew creating an online program would help me leverage the knowledge and Divine Wisdom I'd gathered throughout the years, so I could share it more broadly and meaningfully with others.

But despite all the studying I did and the tools I learned, I never felt as though I could actually create it. I wasn't sure how or where to begin, and I wondered whether what I had to say was enough to put into a program. I worried people would judge me… that they wouldn't consider me qualified to teach on this topic.

Still, I knew it would be worth the risk.

I enrolled in Alina Vincent's Rising Star's Mastermind, which gave me the confidence and tools I needed to create my program. It's simple and to the point, which is the way I like to learn.

I created my program, **Divine Wisdom: Your Divine Connection to Discover Crystal Clear Answers to Your Life Questions.**

One of the most powerful lessons I learned during this process is that I could leverage all my experience (in project management and information technology), education, and gifts to create a program; I wasn't simply selling information… I was selling my unique perspective and take on the Divine Wisdom, and I had a tangible way to showcase and maximize my expertise.

Creating and teaching my program also boosted my confidence. Up until then, I'd never openly talked about the spirituality, or the Divine, or the Creator, or my approach to all of it, because I thought I would be judged. Going through this process allowed me to find my voice and connect with people who needed to hear this message.

Of course, in my case, the creation of Divine Wisdom program was the first step in leveraging my time.

Soon, though, I realized that the potential "reusability" of each piece of the program created even more opportunities for larger-scale leverage. Each time I launched a newer version of the program, the process was a little faster and easier; I reused what I'd prepared, adjusted the content based on feedback from participants, and ran it again. And with all the new channels and offerings constantly evolving online, I could also reuse marketing copy, social media posts, and emails (with some slight adjustments).

Now, if I need to pull a specific piece of content to share with a client, I can; it's already there! If I plan a speaking engagement or interview, I have something written already. I don't have to reinvent the wheel.

Also, I can break my program apart and sell it in separate, standalone pieces, which increases my passive income and enables me to meet people where they are (some prefer to start with one concept at a time in smaller steps).

The result of going through the process of putting my knowledge and expertise into leveraging with an online program is that I now have plenty of time and financial freedom, and I'm enjoying every minute of my life and family!

I have been able to nurture my passion for travel by journeying all over the world: North America (including

Hawaii), Europe, Australia, New Zealand, South America, Asia (i.e., India) and Africa are next!

I live in a beautiful, custom-built home mortgage-free. This is a remarkable personal accomplishment, given my bankruptcy thirty years ago.

And I know I'm changing the world (and on a bigger scale than I originally thought possible) by leveraging my experience, education, gifts, and resources to teach more people.

In fact, one of my clients, Shannon, spoke to the benefits of the work we did together:

Shannon came to me two-and-a-half years ago in the midst of a spiritual reawakening.

"I was very lost, and heartbroken," she said.

Her life was in transition. She'd just finished university and started her career as a nurse (in which she encounters lots of dense energy), and she was also going through a breakup. Her sister found me online, and Shannon booked her first session.

She would later say, "Throughout the years with Carmen, I have healed many issues with her assistance. There was a lot of dense, dark energy that manifested in different ways in my life, which Carmen helped me release and heal. She is the first healer I have encountered who I felt at ease with and totally comfortable talking to. Carmen has helped me heal depression, food allergies, relationship issues, and financial issues."

More recently, Shannon enrolled in my Divine Wisdom program.

While she used to come home from her work drained and burned out and continually booked sessions with me to rebalance her energy, she now practices what she learned during the program to realign her energy and is better able to repel or diffuse negative energy she encounters at work.

Her friends have even commented that she radiates positivity!

"My life continues to blossom each day into something more beautiful," she said. "Even if something negative occurs, I can quickly recover and thrive from the situation. I feel a deeper connection to Creator, and I notice how quickly I manifest things in my life."

As I've mentioned, my mission is to help people like Shannon—and you—reconnect to their Divine Wisdom to find their own Divine Path to accomplish their mission. I'd like to share an exercise to help you do just that—so you can experience greater peace, confidence, and certainty about what you want and where you want your life to go.

Exercise: The Energy of the "I AM"

First, your belief in a higher power—something bigger than humans that created this Universe—and the desire to connect to this Divine source are critical to your ability to make an impact in your own life and the world.

Worldwide, people refer to this Divine source as God, Allah, Buddha, Shiva, Goddess, Jesus, Yahweh, Creator, or Divine Source. It doesn't matter what you choose to call it … as long as you're willing to open yourself to a connection with it.

According to scripture, the words "I AM" is the name of God. Using these words in our daily life opens that connection—the door to life and its natural flow.

Therefore, whenever you begin a sentence with "I AM" (whether you're speaking, thinking, or feeling it), you begin manifesting. You'll create whatever you say next. It's like you're calling in God, every time.

When you say, "I AM not," you shut the door to life and its natural flow.

If you say, "I AM sick," it's as if you're saying, "God (or Creator or Source), I am sick." So God (or the Creator or Source) will send you more sickness.

On the other hand, if you say, "I AM healthy," God (or the Creator or Source) will send you more health.

That being said, be strict with your thoughts and the way you express them. We are all energy. Your thoughts and words are energy, too, and they matter. Also, be persistent and have faith that the Divine *will* act. Be careful, too. If you think hard about what you want for a few seconds or a minute or two, and then afterward secretly stew in your head that it will never come to pass, then it is that last persistent belief that will resonate more.

With every thought you have and every word you speak, you send energy out to that Divine source... and that Divine source sends it back to you (in this sense, you really do reap what you sow!).

The exercise, then, is to practice crafting "I AM" statements that will generate more of what you want in your life.

Step 1. Consider the thoughts you've had recently: What are you attracting into your life? Is it positive? Negative? Is it what you really want?

If it is, great! Keep up the good work.

Step 2. If not, reconstruct your thoughts and words to ensure you're sowing what you want to reap.

Throughout my life, I've experienced plenty of turmoil. But by connecting with my Divine Wisdom, I've been able to cultivate a sense of peace and wellbeing—and purpose.

And, with the help of my online program, I'm living my Divine Mission with certainty and peace.

If you've considered creating content you can leverage, I want you to know that it's worth it.

I wish I'd known about Alina's program-creation course five years ago when I first thought about creating a source of passive income. Not only are the steps in the course so easy to follow I can apply them in many upcoming projects, but they also include what you need to leverage your time, money, energy, and resources.

***

Carmen Gélinas, MBA, is an international speaker/teacher as well as a Spiritual Teacher, Energy Healer, and certified

Leverage Your Expertise

Science ThetaHealing® Instructor/Practitioner. She guides her clients to reconnect with their spirituality and Divine Wisdom, so they can find their own Divine Path and accomplish their mission. With more than 30 years of experience in various public service roles, she understands that life has many caveats, and not all of us feel fully equipped to manage them. By combining her education, expertise, and gifts—natural intuition and a warm disposition—with her work, Carmen hopes to help people find peace, confidence, and certainty about what they want to achieve and where they want to go in life. You can learn more about her here: www.letstalkcoach.com.

Get Carmen's free gift …

Divine Wisdom Meditation to explore and deepen your connection with the Divine, here:

LeverageYourExpertiseBook.com/gifts

Chapter 11
Numbers Busy Business Owners Can Count On
by Marie Gibson

It may be surprising to hear that, despite being an online accounting educator and rescuer, I *disliked* numbers and bookkeeping for years! Yes… you read that correctly. I actually had a love/hate affair with my numbers. And I was my own worst enemy—just like many of the business owners I help! I was a frustrated procrastinator who shoved all invoices and receipts into a shoebox, while ultimately spending days, evenings, and weekends agonizing over what seemed so difficult and time-consuming at the time.

When finally forced into doing the data entry, I would. But even after years of running businesses, I honestly still thought accounting was a necessary evil dreamed up by the government to force us business owners into unhappiness!

I loved running and managing my retail stores through the years—a fabric and craft store, a quilting store, a restaurant, and a shopping mall. I loved the customers, the sales, the marketing, the ordering, the displays, and managing the employees. I totally loved the entrepreneurial kingdom that comes with daily contact with the retail public—except for numbers. However, that deep-seated dislike came to a screeching halt one very tragic evening four days before Christmas, twenty years ago.

I was sharing a home with my fiancée, Stephen, and his son in a small town where one of my retail stores was located; the other store was a two-hour drive away. I regularly commuted between the two locations to manage them and keep them running effectively. My time was at a premium.

Stephen had invited me to spend the evening with them, decorating the tree, wrapping presents, and simply enjoying the holiday season. I regret to this day that I said, "No… I have paperwork and bookkeeping to take care of…"—the perpetual bane of all business owners. That night, Stephen passed away from an unexpected heart attack at 42, and I became my son's legal guardian over that Christmas holiday.

This event changed my life and the way I was forced to approach my businesses. It motivated me to learn how to build and use business systems and numbers to cut expenses to bare bones and "get 'er done"—meaning, whatever it was that needed doing, I needed it done faster, quicker, easier, and more efficiently. After all, as you can imagine, my time was at an even bigger premium than before, and while my business had always earned a profit, it wasn't that big. I now had a household and a son in high school to support.

My employees rallied and helped me learn; we created reports and used software to analyze our sales, our merchandise, and our customers, focusing on those that were most profitable, and **we learned to run our business like a business—using our numbers.**

While I would not wish this experience on anyone, it was a big turning point for how I ran my businesses. It was when I became a "real" business owner! To stay solvent and to support my son, I *had* to know my numbers; I *had* to build systems that made my life easier. I had to earn a profit!

I knew the mental shift that was required, and by making it, my business acumen changed forever! In retrospect, I see that this shift happens when business owners realize that they can use their numbers for easier decision-making.

Within a year of losing my significant other, I was offered a position with a microlender traveling statewide to teach new entrepreneurs how to create their business plans, apply for loans, read their numbers, and make money! It was a perfect fit; I loved the transformation our clients experienced, and I learned to teach budgeting and planning in a totally non-traditional way—a way that busy business owners could understand and embrace.

After surviving that first year, new opportunities were offered to me, and I have since focused on sharing my knowledge and expertise with other business owners—so they too can learn to embrace and love their numbers!

When I say that it's my mission to see the "lightbulb turn on" in my clients' eyes, it truly is!

The next year, I accepted a teaching position at Western Nevada College, and ultimately met and married a wonderful gentleman a few years afterward. I continued teaching several business classes over the years, including several semesters in QuickBooks accounting software.

A few years later, our state university, UNR, reached out, and I accepted a position with them teaching Accounting and Information Systems classes. This is where I met Alina Vincent, who at that time was an instructional designer for the university. She offered her help during my first year, teaching me so much about the technology that was required to educate large, lecture-sized classes. I soon learned to love teaching in the online environment, and eventually, earned my doctorate in online learning issues for accounting students.

After several years of full- and part-time teaching for the university, I started consulting again—this time, helping business owners learn QuickBooks. I left the university and partnered with a bookkeeper to create a new business that would help business owners with their accounting needs or with learning QuickBooks.

During that time, I worked with an online coach, developed webinars, free handouts, and wrote books—basically, I created an online store in conjunction with my business. Looking back, this store and the methodology was a bit piecemeal and not very effective. Sometimes, we focused our marketing on one-on-one clients; occasionally, we would take a stab at marketing online. The idea and promise of the online store and offering webinars just didn't materialize the way I had originally intended. We didn't know how to leverage our business.

My business partner and I eventually decided to divide the business, and I returned again to the one-on-one client work I love so much! However, I very quickly bumped up against that same constraining factor again—time limitations.

There is a specific number of hours in a day that I can work. There are only so many clients I can help within those hours. Deep in my heart, I knew that what I share is extremely valuable to business owners. And I knew I could help so many more if I implemented my ideas about leveraging my time.

It was in early spring of 2020 that I bumped into Alina again. I had lost track of her over the years and was thrilled when she invited me to join one of her online events. I jumped at the chance to reconnect with her and see how she had created and leveraged her successful online business since I had last seen her. I was delighted to learn she was helping entrepreneurs like myself to create online programs and use Facebook to connect with new clients!

And there it was:

I realized by creating online programs, I could actually provide a service that would help business owners understand what accounting is and how to build their own basic system. The programs would lead them to embracing their numbers by showing them how easy it truly is, and that they can take charge of their numbers and run their business profitably, easily, quickly, and efficiently.

One of my initial programs, **Accounting Made Simple for Busy Business Owners**, enables participants to push their feelings of ineptness aside and build their confidence in using their numbers to make decisions. The program is designed especially for busy business owners whose time is a premium. It heralds back to a time of my emotional and physical survival—a time when I was forced into learning about business numbers in a no-nonsense way—a time when I *had* to use my numbers to run my business wisely!

Like all new endeavors, this one didn't come without challenges. My biggest personal challenge during this period of transition is still related to time. I continue to work one-on-one with clients, and I rescue and rehab older horses for a non-profit organization I created three years ago. Occasionally, I feel like I'm not progressing fast enough in certain undertakings. It is then that I have to remind myself of all that I have accomplished in this most recent year! I have launched three programs, created an online classroom environment using Learning Management software, built a Facebook group, designed an in-home recording studio, re-designed and built my website, started a YouTube channel, written several guest articles, participated in the Big Results ToolKit Giveaway, *and* removed my fear of FB Live conversations.

So many positives have come out of my experience creating online programs. The feeling is amazing when you are serving others in a capacity that inspires them! That strong connection to others' success brings overwhelming joy to my personal life!

I've also leveraged my knowledge and expertise by taking my two-day Intensive QuickBooks Workshop that I had been teaching in a university classroom and converting it to over 40 videos, breaking them into two distinct programs: one for the online version of the QuickBooks software; the other for those using the desktop or Mac versions.

My online programs are helping me shift from the traditional delivery method of one-on-one consulting to modern delivery methods and channels, thus allowing me to help additional clients. Plus, using the energy from videos is an amazingly effective tool in sharing my knowledge with others. And the comradery with my counterparts in

Alina's program-creation group provided me a great deal of personal connection that I needed while working on my business.

Creating the programs also allowed me to think through how to share the joy of numbers with online entrepreneurs—I teach in a very non-traditional fashion, using imagery (instead of debits and credits) to convey the basic concepts of accounting and numbers, so this emotional draw toward a non-traditional delivery method aligns well with my intentions.

Business numbers should be fast, quick, and easy, and leave the business owners feeling pleased with the knowledge gleaned from their reports. It warms my heart to be able to help more people get there! Here are a few examples of what my clients experienced when they learned to use their numbers:

One client, Anne Hession, broke through a mindset barrier that had been created from an experience with a grade-school teacher. She took charge of her accounting, learned to read her reports, and is using her numbers to make great decisions that save her money!

Catherine Eardley felt she was almost drowning, because she didn't understand the language of accounting or know how to read her numbers and use the information. After working together, she's started working smarter, not harder, and now knows how to read her reports and get numbers that help her and her husband make decisions quickly and easily!

Another client, a construction contractor, Brian, had been paying multiple online subscriptions for online app services that his company used—but several of the subscriptions were for previous employees whose email addresses were no longer current! He had inadvertently continued paying for these subscriptions even after the employees had left. He only discovered this when he learned to read his numbers!

Another business owner, Judy, found that they were able to prepare their loan application for the PPP stimulus funding in just a few easy steps, because they had all their numbers at their fingertips! They were so thankful and appreciative.

An additional business owner, Rachel, makes candles and soaps on weekends. Before working together, she focused on the ones that sold the most. When she learned to look at her numbers differently, she shifted her focus to the products that sold for higher profit. She then spent less time on her creations and tripled her profit in less than three months!

As you can see, once you can read your numbers and feel comfortable with your reports, you can turn chaos to clarity easily and quickly!

If you are an entrepreneur who doesn't love numbers, or you can relate to my clients, keep reading for a few easy steps that will help you take control of your accounting while taking your first step toward loving your numbers! These basic steps may seem so simple, you might be tempted to skip them. However, they are the foundation to building an accounting system that helps you earn more profit!

Exercise: 3 Basic Steps to Simplifying Your Accounting System

Step 1: Separate your business funds from your personal money.

Your business is a pretty big deal, right? It may already be your main source of income for you and your family, or maybe you'd like it to be, soon. It's your professional passion and identity… so give it the respect it deserves! Separate your business and personal finances, and set up a special business bank account for your business. You will save yourself so much time, stress, and expense in the long run, and you will be immensely proud of your professional identity and success. Furthermore, this separation makes tax preparation and any potential audits easier and cleaner.

Step 2: Start keeping your business records.

You'd be amazed by how many business owners don't keep any records of their business finances—no deductible expenses, no reliable income documentation, no consistent way of tracking vendor payments… not even bank statements.

If you have no records of any kind, your business is completely flying blind. Maybe your business started as a hobby or as a side gig, and you've barely made enough income to cover your expenses. Perhaps that suddenly changed, and your business is a real business. If you haven't added any internal support or infrastructure, you've built it without a proper foundation.

If right now you're thinking, "Awesome. I have a shoebox. I give it to my accountant to organize for tax purposes at the end of the year." Well… yes, that is better than not keeping any records at all. It also leads us to our third step!

Step 3: Start organizing your business records.

Ultimately, if you're using shoebox accounting (just tossing in the paperwork and leaving it scrambled), you're sending a message to yourself about your business. You may not yet be treating it as a serious endeavor.

Your next step is to organize your records and start creating reports. You can do this with or without software. As you start organizing your paperwork, it will begin to reveal a story about your business. It's this story, the reports and information, that is so powerful! (And, pragmatically, your tax accountant will charge you a fortune for organizing your shoebox at tax time, so this will save you money in that respect, too!)

Once you have taken these steps, you may wonder when to adopt accounting software, whether it will ultimately complicate or simply your life. and how will it help you create a business you love. Be sure to download my special gift for you below—it's a free training to help you determine whether accounting software can help you leverage your time even more by automating the process.

In conclusion, my best advice for creating a profitable business is to protect your time and learn how to leverage it to maximize your impact on others. Find team members and affiliates who can help you create and promote online programs to leverage your expertise and knowledge. Your efforts will result in numbers you can be proud of!

***

Marie Gibson, an online accounting educator and rescuer,

has a big heart for entrepreneurs and small business owners! She helps them make more money and keep more of it by creating accounting systems that are fast, easy, effective, and accurate. Marie, a member of Intuit's National Trainer Writer Network, built her online business to better serve busy entrepreneurs who need help using their numbers to make decisions—all at an affordable price! Removing stumbling blocks and enabling business owners and entrepreneurs to have successful businesses is the source of Marie's inspiration. She is thrilled to be leveraging her knowledge and expertise into simple, easy-to-understand programs and books which encourage business owners to break through their agony with numbers. When they do, they understand that numbers are their friends! Marie helps business owners KNOW their numbers… and make SMART business decisions! You can learn more about Marie and see her course catalog here: www.Marie-Gibson.com.

Get Marie's free gift …

Signs Your Business Is Ready (or Past Due) for Accounting Software here:

LeverageYourExpertiseBook.com/gifts

Leverage Your Expertise

Chapter 12
Where Leverage Really Starts
by Monica Bijoux

I was 12 years old when I first began to realize my life's calling and discover my purpose.

I remember the moment as if it were yesterday. I watched a news story about an 18-year-old foster child who had aged out of foster care, become homeless, and turned to prostitution to pay her way through college.

Although I was young, I knew what I was watching was not okay, so I made a promise to myself then and there that when I "made it," I would operate a ranch-style foster home where I could take in foster children and rescued animals such as horses and dogs.

These animals and children would teach one another how to trust, and my foster home would be filled with love and learning, so my fosters would know they have choices in life and could be whatever they desired as adults.

That's my big, audacious hair goal (bahg) and one of my "whys." It's the reason behind everything I do, and it—along with an always-present desire to be of service and help people—fueled both my career and entrepreneurial journey.

My other "why" is my daughter. I gave birth to her when I was 17 years old and clueless; however, after overcoming abuse and homelessness, I knew I wanted her to know she could accomplish anything she wanted.

With my bahg and my daughter, I had all the fire and fuel I needed to achieve my life's purpose and goals.

I'm a mental health therapist in the U.S. military, *and* I'm an award-nominated master-level certified business coach and strategist who guides high-achievers and military veterans to become entrepreneurs via my coaching and consulting business, DECIDE TO MOVE LLC. I'm an international bestselling author who has collaborated on four book projects, a Webby Award Honoree for Best Host for my podcast with the same name as my business, a certified anthologist, and an international speaker and trainer. I say what all I do not to brag or boast, but to emphasize how you don't have to allow your past to define you. I do what I do and have accomplished all that I have by being clear on who I am and focused.

It's my passion to help people discover their God-given purpose, and then, to give them the strategies, knowledge, and confidence to live that purpose with excellence… in many cases, through entrepreneurship. I do this by helping my clients identify limiting beliefs that need to be addressed immediately. Then, we begin laying the foundation necessary for them to achieve their business goals.

After I'd spent some time as a coach, I realized that I could reach more people—and help them discover their purpose and live it with excellence—if I created a few online programs.

Choosing the focus of my first program was difficult! I have experience and expertise in a lot of areas, so I had to take a serious self-inventory to dial in on who I truly wanted to serve and which services I wanted to provide. I also had to consider and decide what I desired to be known for and what I wanted to contribute to this world.

I received lots of advice about where to place my focus, but I knew I needed to build the foundation for a business that would make the most of my experiences and passion, and that would pave the way for me to create courses I would want to buy myself.

That's when I had my first "aha!" moment: *I'm a foundation builder.* I thrive when I have a step-by-step strategy based on my personality… and for me, the same applied to creating an online course.

I had to build a foundation based on what I wanted, and then create and teach my courses with that same foundational mindset.

My first program centered around my work as a therapist. Ultimately, it was not what I wanted to be known for, as it focused on trauma work and not business. However, creating this trauma course was an eye-opening experience. I went back to the drawing board and asked myself what was the one question I was constantly asking my coach *and* that my clients were asking me. This is when I realized clients were struggling with the same issue I had when I started, which was knowing how to answer the question "What do I do first?" This is when I determined my next course had to be based on teaching clients how to first build a foundation for their business.

I also learned that I could create a course anytime I wanted using the basics I had already used the first time, and that the course could be taught live (include coaching) or evergreen (where the client goes through the course on his or her own). I discovered that it empowered me to help clients in a more powerful way while safeguarding my time and making more money. Program creation also guided me in developing (and later, improving) a systemized process.

Finally, in creating my foundation course, Client Attraction List Builder, I quickly realized the opportunity for leverage. That is, I could find many uses for the content and process I used for one program… without putting in more time, energy, or money. This was and still is important to me, because with working full-time in the military, having private coaching clients, being a podcast host, and all the other things I do, it's crucial that I use my time and energy efficiently while being effective.

The courses I have created provide exactly what my clients have asked me to teach. The Client Attraction List Builder focuses on helping clients define their niche, audience, and message, create Freebies/Opt-ins based on their ideal client, set up their Customer Relationship Management platform and Scheduler (calendar), write a six-part welcome sequence for new clients, and build their funnels (opt in and consultation) to attract their ideal clients.

The other courses are podcast courses that teach how to start and monetize a podcast and course creation courses that teach how to create an online course, how to create high-ticket offers, and how to write, publish, and monetize a client-attraction book. All are focused on helping my clients build a strong business foundation, attract ideal clients, build their brand, and become more visible and credible while increasing their authority in their market.

Thanks to leveraging with my online program, I have been able to reach more people, watch my clients become successful, and do what I love while I increase my profits!

For example, after creating my program, I built a membership site that I will eventually expand into an academy that I can offer to my clients as one of the ways they can work with me at a higher level. The bonus is that my academy will allow me to make money in my sleep, every month. I can add group coaching to any of my programs or as a special bonus at any time, including if and when I want to increase the value of one of my evergreen courses. I also work one-on-one with private clients and charge a higher price point due to the personalization they receive along with access to additional courses.

My courses have allowed me to turn my experience, passion, and education (resources) into multiple courses that provide value to my clients. I know I am on the right track when my clients are transforming, growing, and developing in their life and business as I imagined they would.

I've also learned how to effectively collaborate with others to enhance my course offerings to leverage through joint venturing. Joint venturing allows me to get in front of other people's audiences and expand my reach.

Along the way, I learned to leverage my own podcast, other people's podcasts, media (magazines, online publishing, and tv appearances), and social media, too.

Since I started leveraging my expertise through various programs and offerings, I've received so many wonderful comments from my clients and customers. To me, they are proof that through my different offerings, I'm still making a significant impact and living my purpose (even though I'm not always working one-on-one with people!).

In fact, one of my clients told me she struggled for more than a year to turn her business idea into a systematic process; after we started working together, she finally had the clarity she needed to create one. Now, she can sleep in peace knowing exactly what she needs to do based on her personality (and not just the next get-rich idea).

Here are just a few comments from other clients, so you can see the results I help them achieve:

"DECIDE TO MOVE LLC is exactly what Monica inspires her audiences to do! Her calm and powerful demeanor makes you feel safe in taking the next step in your business even when you may not know what is coming next. She helped my daughter gain confidence in herself and her business after just one short, powerful conversation. If you are looking for solid tips and guidance that will get you unstuck and making boss moves for your business, DECIDE TO MOVE LLC should be your top choice." – Karen Clark-Reddon

"Brilliant and vibrant expert with deep knowledge about women in transition." – Carol Henry

"An awesome person with a wealth of knowledge to help others. She knows how to help you frame your vision." – Tina Cook

"Monica is full of jewels, nuggets, and expertise. Her wisdom… has grown my email list in a span of one month. There were so many other jewels dropped that have helped my business move to another level. It has moved and grown in an incredible way." – Frances Bailey

"Before talking to Monica, I had so many ideas, I could not figure out where I should start or even how to get started with my business goals. After a free consultation call, I was so clear that I was able to the strategies she gave me and get so much accomplished in just one week. This was all because I was clear and knew exactly what I needed to do. Thank you so much, Monica. You truly are amazing." – Esonija Fulgam

As I mentioned, when I first considered creating a program, the most difficult part for me was to choose what to teach… in other words, to find my genius zone.

If you're anything like I was, and you're embarking on an entrepreneurial journey, you have so many ideas, you may not be sure which one will make the best use of your knowledge and skills *and* the biggest impact.

I encourage you to embrace your past, focus on the lessons you learned along the way, and consider what you can teach others. Your mess is definitely your message!

Build the foundation of your business based on your message by being authentic and true to who you are and what you truly want to do—not on what others say you ought to do.

That being said, I'd like to share with you my four-step process for getting all those ideas out of your head and determining your genius zone:

Step 1. On the left side of your paper, write down all your business ideas.

Step 2. Using a scale of 1-10 (where 1 is uncertain and 10 is your strength), for each of the ideas you wrote down in Step 1, rate yourself on experience, passion, resources, and profitability. Double the value for profitability.

Step 3. Add up the scores for each idea, and you'll discover which is the strongest business option for you.

Step 4. Write down the idea with the highest score; that's your winner!

I'm confident this exercise will provide you with clarity around where to focus on your business; that's the very first step in creating leverage.

One mistake I've seen would-be entrepreneurs make is trying to serve everyone in lots of ways... which is the opposite of leverage. Entrepreneurs often believe that if they don't include everything, they're not going to be able to effectively serve their clients. In fact, the opposite is true. You don't have to include all of your expertise in one product or program.

Narrowing down a specific group of people, their specific struggle, and your specific knowledge and method for helping them solve that struggle will empower you to work more efficiently (and that's the definition of leverage, right?).

So, as you embark on this new phase of your entrepreneurial journey, keep in mind that it's critical to be crystal clear on your niche and audience, the struggle your audience is experiencing, and your message. Only when you know precisely who you serve and communicate to those people in the words that resonate with them can you truly create leverage.

Once you create your first program, the rest falls into place! You'll have the foundation you need to create additional offerings… and the leverage that empowers you to make the biggest possible difference in this world!

***

Monica Bijoux, CEO & Founder of DECIDE TO MOVE LLC, helps high-achievers, especially military veterans, become entrepreneurs by taking ideas and turning them into a successful and thriving business in order to create financial freedom and live a life of purpose. Overcoming a life of abuse and homelessness, Monica, now a licensed psychotherapist and business strategist, uses her decade of experience to help others find the "jewel" inside by creating a personalized systematic strategy using the 12-step model of DECIDE TO MOVE that focuses on transformation, transition, growth, and development. Monica is an international bestselling author, an award-winning podcast host, and an international speaker and trainer. You can learn more about her here: decidetomove.com.

Get Monica's free gift …

Discover Your Genius Zone to get clear on the content to teach in your program based on your own experiences, expertise, and passion, here:

LeverageYourExpertiseBook.com/gifts

Chapter 13
A Twitching-Eared Zebra on the Leading Edge of Change
by Barbara Lawson, FSA, FCIA, MBA

As far back as I can remember, I have always thought ahead. I made choices that allowed me to build the financial life I wanted 20 years into the future. What I am going to share with you today will show you how to set up your financial well-being for the next 20 years, too.

Growing up, we looked ahead as a family. School was our first job, and my dad made numbers fun.

I remember holding my first bank book when I was six. Dad showed me how he deposited the government baby bonus given to my mother each month into my bank account. He also explained how they had taken out a life insurance policy on my life when I was born. The only withdrawals from my account were to pay the annual premium each year.

Like many firstborns, I loved teaching my siblings in ways my mother had taught me. At a young age, I also learned to watch over my brother and sister like a twitching-eared zebra protecting the herd.

When it was time to choose a career, I chose the actuarial profession. It aligned with my love of math, my natural draw to look at trends long into the future, and my interest in protecting individuals.

For those of you who may not know, actuaries assess risk. We do things like project mortality, interest, and expenses far into the future to price insurance and pension products. Insurance protects people from the risk of passing away without leaving enough assets to take care of loved ones. Pensions provide some security against running out of money during retirement.

Over the years, I have often found myself on the leading edge of change. After I was hired by an insurance company, I realized I was one of the first women in their actuarial program. There were no women-held senior management positions in the company at all.

In time, I moved away from doing technical work and focused on business strategy and management. Over an 18-year period, I worked on many projects that positioned the company to remain one of the top insurance companies in Canada after consolidation of the insurance industry. Many of those projects were lots of fun for me—like creating defined contribution pension plans, starting a mutual fund company, and evaluating the world-wide IT needs of an international corporation.

1998 was a challenging year for the insurance industry and for me. One day, I was called into a meeting and told my services were no longer required. In an instant, my 20-year career with the company was over. In the blink of an eye, a large part of my world was completely replaced by loss of income, stability, my identity, structure, and community. They were all gone. Perhaps you can relate.

I went home.

I took stock.

And from that point on, I gave myself permission to only do the things I love to do.

Out of this unimaginable disruption, I became determined to learn how to create work and a life I love. I set up my financial well-being for the next 20 years. Here's how I did it:

1. I leveraged my natural gifts.

I decided to leverage my natural gift of bringing out people's potential and build a business around it. I learned of the fledgling coaching profession and knew it would be a perfect fit. Having my own business (now Barbara Lawson Coaching Inc.) and being my own boss was the way forward.

The thought of building my own business was daunting. I had absolutely no idea how to find clients or sell. I started by setting a goal of covering my business and living expenses. Then, wouldn't you know, the universe provided. My hairdresser said he knew of an amazing networking group that would be a really good fit for me. I joined the group, and through its members, found business owners and executives to work with right away. My tagline was, "Create the life you love—if not now… when?"

2. I leveraged my time and that of my clients.

Within a couple of years, my husband and I found ourselves the happy parents of twin little girls. I created a perfect mix of serving one-on-one clients, bringing up our daughters, and travelling. Working with clients three days a week, three weeks out of four, created a very easy rhythm for my clients and me. One week off each month allowed time for my clients to integrate their learning. In five-week months, my husband and I were able to take two or three consecutive weeks for travel with the family. Working over the phone meant clients were location-independent, which allowed me to work from the cottage all summer.

3. I leveraged my thinking mindset.

I have an ability to look ahead far further than most people, and I take action on what I see far ahead of most people, too.

Using methodology similar to that of the pricing model I used as an actuary, I created my own Vision Alignment System. I work with every client to anchor their vision or life purpose in long-term societal and business trends. I help them identify the skill sets they will need down the road. By taking action to grow these strategic skill sets immediately, they can proactively position their businesses to be ahead of the curve. By taking action today, they can leverage all their tomorrows.

And for the next 13 years, I brought in consistent income every single month. I was living the life I loved, and I was helping others do the same. I was very grateful.

In the words of one of my clients:

"Sales increased from $1 million to $4 million within the first six months of my working with you, all while I was working four days per week. Your combination of intelligence, real-world experience, deep caring for people, and a mathematical mind is very rare. Your ability to take in copious amounts of information, extraordinarily quickly gain insight into complex human situations, and rapidly come up with a variety of solutions within a human context is an amazing gift." - A.T. - CEO, software company

However, from 2008 on, things started to change.

My business wasn't growing the way I expected it to.

Again, I took stock.

I started to realize I needed to get paid more or work with more clients. But there were several problems with that:

1. I didn't know how to get paid more.

2. I already had a full practice. I couldn't take on any more clients.

3. I couldn't see how working with groups would get the depth of transformation I could get working one-on-one.

4. I couldn't see how working with groups would lead to passive income, which was one of my business goals.

5. I realized if I were to lose everything now or at any time in the future, I wouldn't have enough lifetime left to replace the lost assets in the slow way I had accumulated them in the past.

Guided by my Vision Alignment System, I invested in coaching programs to add skill sets to my toolbox. I learned how to increase what I charged to bring in more income. I studied how to build leveraged businesses and make leveraged sales. I learned how to create an infusion of income into a business at will.

Even so, finding a way forward took a lot longer than I expected.

During this same timeframe, I experienced more personal disruptions, each larger than the previous. They included economic downturns, stock market disruptions, the loss of my husband's job, and looking after my elderly parents. The unpredictability of elder care meant giving up my one-on-one clients.

Having experienced these disruptions, I started to question my ability to withstand other large potential disruptions to my cash flow during my upcoming retirement. Think: another pandemic, rapid inflation, unknown long-term care needs or access to out-of-country medical procedures. This led me to the most important aspect of handling unanticipated disruptions.

4. I leveraged my relationship with money.

When working with my clients to create the work and life they love, I learned major breakthroughs happen when people become conscious of their underlying natural instincts around money. I call these instincts "invisible money drivers." We are naturally drawn to either save or spend, to make a lot of money or not, and to be open or secretive about money. It doesn't matter if we are savers or spenders. It takes knowing how to consciously make money, spend it, and keep it in order to have financial freedom.

An important insight I gained working with my clients was that even though I know how to save and invest money myself, I couldn't blindly teach the strategies that worked for me, because my way isn't the optimal path for everyone. I have to work with clients to create their own customized plans to make and keep more money. These plans must be aligned with their own invisible money drivers.

To address my concerns about handling any future disruptions to cash flow during retirement, I concluded I would have to be far more in control of making, spending, and keeping money than I had planned. And I would need to do it long past the traditional retirement age of 65.

Taking an inventory of the skill sets I had collected over the intervening years and guided by my Vision Alignment System, **I decided to build my own leveraged online business to contribute to my family's financial security. I decided to gain the peace of mind financial freedom brings and help other business owners do the same.**

Within six months of the start of the COVID-19 pandemic, I heard of Alina Vincent and her experience developing online university-level programs. Surprisingly, students using these programs experienced more impactful, individualized transformation than when interacting with professors in person. This meant Alina's programs addressed the concerns I had about the effectiveness of working with groups and also had the potential for passive income. I had found something I wanted to explore to create my own leveraged business.

Because understanding money is pivotal to having both the work and the life you love, I decided to create a five-week online program called Money Mindset Makeover. This program would help business owners create their customized roadmaps for making and keeping more money.

Getting my pilot program off the ground was a lot easier than I expected. I leveraged my already-proven system I use with my one-on-one clients to create each of the modules, and I filled it by simply reaching out to business owners in my network. Six people signed up at $197 each for a total of $1,182 within six days of my announcing the program.

I leveraged time, effort, and resources during the creation of the program itself, and I learned a lot along the way.

For example, simplification is essential for marketing online. I chose to solve one problem (money mindset) for a single target market (business owners).

By selling my program before I even started to create the modules, I knew it was something the participants wanted.

I was also able to adjust future modules as I received feedback on each module I delivered. Finally, the Q&A sessions gave me an opportunity to see how powerful my content was.

One of the biggest benefits has been the impact of being invited to participate in other joint venture communities. People really responded to the topic of money mindset, and my referral partners were excited to promote it.

And, as my program evolved, so did my confidence.

Here's what some of my program participants had to say about their experience:

"A single exercise drove home for me the simple, simple concept that life is much more than existence. We all know that, yet we get up in the morning, go to work, get home at night, go to bed, and we exist. This exercise made me aware of the need to look at money and wealth in relation to my life as a whole. Money Mindset Makeover is a program for business owners who want to take their finances seriously. Whether you are a seasoned business owner taking a leadership position in your own business or someone just starting out, this is a program to help train your mind to think about money." - Geoffrey Gonneau - Home Inspector, Insurance Dispute Mediator

"The templates, exercises, and handouts helped open my eyes to my true power to create wealth for my clients. This program

is for long-time business owners and those just starting out, because how we think about money dictates our success." - Jeff Gregory - Financial Planner

"I like the fact that I can refer to this resource again and again. If you have not talked to Barbara about your business and how she can help you strategize and take whatever you are doing to the next level, you are doing yourself a disservice." - Leo Johnston - House Painter, Artist

"Money Mindset Makeover gave me an alternative approach to understand how I and others think about money. I was also able to use this program toward my continuing professional development requirements." - Brian Jenkins, FSA, FCIA - Actuary

Maybe you can relate to my story, or to what one of my clients said above about creating the work and life we love. If so, I'd love to offer the following exercise to get you thinking about how you might leverage your expertise to create the work and life you love, too.

Exercise: Take Stock – 4 Steps to Start Creating the Work and Life YOU Love

Write down your answers to all the following questions:

1. Leverage Your Natural Gifts. Was there something you loved to do as a child? What have you naturally done that you love doing? Do you enjoy singing? Taking care of others? Writing? Teaching your siblings? Could you leverage any of these interests to become self-employed? Could you orient your business around something you love?

2. Leverage Your Thinking Mindset. Do you have some knowledge, skills, technical expertise, and/or content of your own that you could leverage? I was able to create my Vision Alignment System based on an actuarial pricing model. Then, I based the modules of my Money Mindset Makeover online course on my Vision Alignment System. Perhaps there is some strategic thinking or mindset that you can build upon.

3. Leverage Your Time. Give yourself permission to live your life with no regrets. What does your ideal day/week/month/year look like? How can you leverage your time to create the lifestyle you want? Perhaps you would like to go to the office four days a week like my client, A.T., and work on a passion project one day a week. Or perhaps you might do something like I did, and work three weeks out of four. Perhaps you could take two or three weeks off during a five-week month so you can travel with your family.

4. Leverage Your Relationship with Money. This is an area to go gently with yourself. There is no right or wrong. Remember, it doesn't matter if you are a spender or a saver. Where do you find it easy to spend money? Perhaps it is easy to spend money on others but not on yourself. Maybe you find it easy to save. Think about what my clients Geoff, Leo, Jeff, and Brian shared about money and business. What is one thing you would like to change around your relationship with money?

My clients who really engage with these questions get clear insights about themselves. They find exactly what they need to start building the work and life they love. This is my wish for you, too.

People sometimes ask for my advice when it comes to creating leverage in their business with an online program. I offer the following three points:

1. Choose a topic for your program that is foundational to the work you do with your clients and something you want to continue to study.

2. Find mentors. Getting the right mentors is critical. It is important to find ones who are the right fit for you—who listen to you and bring out your very best.

3. Leverage the expertise of your mentors. Creating your program is just the first step. To scale to the six-figure level, there are a lot of moving parts to put into place. These include activities such as:

- building your community and lists,

- clarifying your message,

- increasing your visibility,

- adjusting marketing and sales,

- adding technology, and

- finding joint venture partners to help with promotion.

It is so important to have mentors to guide and support you to break through the barriers and answer your questions along the way.

I have learned and grown so much on my journey to create the work and life I love! I have found building a leveraged business using an online program is a wonderful way to make and keep more money. After reading my story, I hope you feel inspired to create a leveraged business, too.

LeverageYourExpertiseBook.com/gifts

***

Before starting her coaching business in 2000, Barbara L. Lawson, FSA, FCIA, MBA, worked for international corporations in the financial services, telecommunication, and food industries. Her passion for helping people realize their full potential and her desire to build a business that supports family life inspired her to become a coach. Barbara has combined her experience as an actuary and business strategist with 20 years as a business and executive coach to create the Money Mindset Makeover online program to help business owners make and keep more money in these uncertain times. Barbara is a Fellow of the Society of Actuaries and of the Canadian Institute of Actuaries and a graduate of The Ivey School of Business (University of Western Ontario) and of Coach University. She lives with her family in Toronto, Canada. You can learn more about her here: www.barbaralawsoncoaching.com.

Get Barbara's free gift …

Discover Your Invisible Money Drivers to make and keep more money and jumpstart your journey to create the work and life you love, here:

LeverageYourExpertiseBook.com/gifts

Chapter 14
Unlock & Live Your Creative Dreams
by Sam Whitesell

My story—or, more specifically, that of my business—begins when I was six years old.

There are many things I considered fun: riding my bike, doing jumps and wheelies on it, creating long narrative stories with my twin brother, skating on a nearby pond, building with Legos, and exploring the large expanses of nature around my childhood home in upstate New York.

What did *you* like to do when you were young?

I spent a lot of time tinkering around on the piano, which provided me with a sense of accomplishment, deep enjoyment, and inspiration. Both of my parents played, and I loved listening to music of all kinds.

As I grew older, I became more skilled, versatile, and aware in my playing. Making music with my friends and my brother was one of my favorite pastimes.

But years later, I realized I'd lost that fun and sense of accomplishment around the piano that I'd experienced as a child.

I can't really put my finger on exactly when or how, but I imagine years of rigorous formal training, ongoing critical feedback from teachers and peers, and my own internal insecurities and perfectionism dimmed the joy of tickling those black and white keys.

The good news is that once I realized that the joy was gone, and, more importantly, that I missed the connection I once had with making music, *I was able to make a conscious decision to reclaim* what I had lost!

That's what led me to my life's work: helping adults rediscover their joy and connection with the piano.

The road to where I am now has been an interesting one… and I believe you might be able to relate!

When I first moved to Vermont, it took me a few years to build up my teaching studio. But I eventually reached the point where I was working beyond capacity, teaching 30 students (mostly children) one-on-one every week while also working a part-time job as a church musician *and* performing gigs in the community as a freelance pianist.

Needless to say, I was working more than full-time, and because of some of the performances I was involved in, I often worked odd hours, too! And even though my rates were comparable to (if not a little higher than) the "going" rate in town, and my schedule was full, I wasn't earning the money I wanted to.

It didn't take long to realize what I really wanted and needed—**to be able to earn more money** (I knew I'd hit a ceiling when it came to one-on-one teaching) and **get my schedule under control** (work regular and fewer hours).

Although I knew I offered something special in terms of how I ran my studio and taught my students, I wasn't sure how to define it. I seemed to "get" the students other teachers couldn't relate to; I could help them feel comfortable about themselves while honoring their unique learning styles, and I was always excited to help them learn the specific music they wanted to play—but I didn't know how to express all that in my marketing.

After lots of soul searching and contemplating, I realized that until we addressed the mindset "stuff" that sabotaged my students' efforts, we couldn't really work on the mechanics of playing piano, let alone the whole creative side. When it came to my adult students, many had actual trauma around past musical experiences, and that trauma had stuck with them. A few of my adult students had already identified some of these mindset issues in themselves when they came to me, whereas with others, I helped them through the discovery process. But for each and every student, I found I was naturally skillful at *supporting* them.

Meanwhile, I was working on my own personal growth and spiritual seeking, and I learned some interesting things about myself: I'm strongly empathic, highly intuitive, and unusually creative. More recently, my doctor diagnosed me with ADHD (which is associated with the above positive traits, plus having a special knack for big-picture thinking and a natural gift for counseling).

Suddenly, the journey of my career as a pianist and teacher was making more sense! I had an affinity for teaching kids with ADHD tendencies (probably because I had them myself) and adults who didn't take well to traditional piano lessons when they were younger. I had struggled with various mindset issues around playing (stage fright, low self-esteem, taking the judgement of peers and authority figures too seriously, and more), so I could readily relate to these same challenges when I'd encounter them in the students I was attracting.

Back when I was in university studying music for my bachelor's degree, many years before these powerful realizations were occurring, I developed tendonitis in my arms from acute tension. Because of this and other converging factors at the time, I made the difficult decision shortly after graduating to take a hiatus from music in the hopes of my arms healing.

During that hiatus, I also wanted to get more in touch with myself, the world, and nature. So, I worked on a few small organic farms and at a spiritual retreat center, not mentioning my background in music. I played piano in secret sometimes, and when people finally discovered I was a pianist and recognized my talent for it, they strongly encouraged me to pursue it again.

At that point, I was really itching to get back to the keyboard again, and to teach.

I decided to go back to school to earn my master's degree in piano to continue advancing my skills and get in touch with my musically expressive self again. Also, I received specialized support in a couple of powerful modalities that helped loosen me up physically and put me much more in touch with my body, which made it easier to enjoy piano playing, as well as other daily activities, pain-free.

My goal at that point was to play easily, efficiently, effortlessly, and with as much soul as I could muster.

I started playing piano for churches, choirs, and solo instrumentalists and singers, and then began teaching students one-on-one.

I learned about the **importance of leverage**… specifically, about finding my niche. It became clear mine was working with kids with ADHD tendencies and adults, who, like me, used to play the piano and were looking for support in enjoying doing so again.

Which brings me back to that "ceiling" I mentioned earlier. My teaching practice had filled up, and I knew it was time to leverage.

Teaching online seemed like a great option, and I sensed that teaching adults online would be easier than teaching kids online.

However, I honestly didn't believe that teaching piano online was even possible, much less teaching groups online. Plus, I didn't know anything about marketing or online marketing.

Then, the pandemic hit.

Overnight, I *had* to transition from one-on-one, in-person teaching to one-on-one online teaching. I was surprised at how quickly I was able to learn the technology, and how effectively I was still able to teach.

And that was the impetus I needed to finally take action and create leverage in my business.

In late April 2020, I attended Alina Vincent's High Profit Programs event and saw the huge potential for shift and leverage in my business. I mapped out my pilot program, and then joined Alina's Rising Stars Mastermind in May.

With lots of support, I delivered the first version of my online program, **Back to the Piano: Play It Again With Sam!** in mid-October 2020 to 12 students. The results were outstanding! I successfully followed up that pilot run of the program with a Group Masterclass. Three people enrolled, and it went even better than I'd hoped. I've since successfully run the program a second time, and I now plan to offer it multiple times a year.

The process of creating an online program forced me to systematize my foundational approach and materials and sequence them in a logical and meaningful way. Although I'd sensed this implicitly, I realized that each pianist uses the same handful of tools at their own level … and that's when I was able to explicitly identify and teach those tools in a brand-new, cohesive, and powerful way.

I filled my first program at a very low intro price ($97) but then ran it for the second time for the much higher price of $497. At that point, I effectively doubled my one-on-one fees overnight. I'm confident now about increasing the investment for the program to $697 and then $997 going forward.

I have chosen to now focus specifically on group courses and coaching, as I enjoy it, and it feels like an effective leveraging strategy. Working one-to-ten or one-to-twenty is a hugely efficient use of my time, and my students receive enormous benefits, too. In addition to my teaching, they also get group support, community, camaraderie, feedback, and momentum in much bigger ways than they would working one-on-one.

Since discovering how to leverage my expertise, I now have an online program and two complimentary live workshops under my belt that I can offer any time, multiple follow-up programs in the works, and more ideas for further workshops and possibly even retreats… the beauty is, there are *so* many ways to leverage my business and make a difference in the lives of even more people!

As other business owners have heard about my program, we've begun to network. I'm excited to be on other people's interviews and podcasts, and about setting up my own online community where I can invite other guests to share with my tribe.

And that's not even the best of it: the personal growth I've experienced during this process is opening me up to new levels of confidence and ability in my personal and professional life! I feel more focused in my work and the value I provide.

I am now poised—personally and professionally—to step out and become visible on a global scale… helping more students achieve life-changing transformation through their piano playing and creative self-expression.

The story of my student, Brian, serves as a great example of the work my students and I do together:

A recent retiree, Brian has always enjoyed singing and playing guitar as a singer-songwriter. He's also taken lessons and played piano a couple of times throughout his life, but never felt the same fluidity he did with his guitar playing.

He sought my help with the mental and physical tools that would help him fully relax into the instrument and flow of the music. Through our work together, he was able to access a focused meditative state at the keyboard, which empowered him to forget (for a time) about the stressors in his everyday life and the world.

Because he felt supported in playing music he loves on piano—classical, classic pop from the 70s, and his own compositions—he was finally able to enjoy performing piano for others … first for his wife, then for friends and family, and eventually for the community during a beloved coffeehouse function at his church, where he fulfilled a personal dream: playing piano and singing at the same time.

It was so rewarding for him, and now he's working on a rock band recording project with old friends… another dream!

Now, I'd like to share with you a brief meditation designed to help you access and reconnect with the creative expression you enjoyed as a child.

It will help you feel great about your life, relieve stress and anxiety, increase productivity, and find joy and confidence in the creative process.

Exercise: Discover Your Creative Spark!

Step 1. Take 15 minutes to yourself. Let yourself relax into a quiet, meditative space, and think back to the creative activities you enjoyed as a child… what was it? Was it art, music, sports, writing, play acting, or just running up and down the street? Is there something you used to love doing that's now just a memory? When you think about it, what comes up for you? Do you remember how you used to joyfully spend your time before becoming saddled with the many responsibilities of adulthood? What was your favorite thing to do, and your favorite way to be while doing all these things? Take some time to feel into this.

Step 2. Think about a role model or teacher who inspired your younger self in your favorite form of creative self-expression. Was it a performer who enchanted you? A favorite musician or singer? Was it an artist? An author? A parent or a friend? Your favorite actor or actress? Was it an athlete? Who inspired you?

Step 3. What impact did your role models have on you? What do you notice? What do you remember? What sensations are coming up for you? Are you getting in touch with an experience or a sensation you'd forgotten? In what ways did your role models impact you? Feel deeply into this and simply notice what you notice.

Step 4. What was an early creative experience you enjoyed being part of? It might be writing a specific written piece while holed up alone in a quiet place, or fully exploring and experiencing your body's storytelling capacities through a particular dance performance or experience. Or maybe it was feeling blissfully in tune with your body and in flow while maneuvering athletically on a field out in the wild. Close your eyes if you need to. How deeply can you recall and feel into the experience? What feelings surface? Do you feel anything now that you've been missing, without realizing it? Stay with this experience for as long as you wish.

Step 5. Gently and slowly come out of your experience, and spend some time noticing what came to you. What did it stir up inside you? What creative activity came up for you? How long has it been since you've played at it? What can you do right now to start doing more of that?

Step 6. If it's possible to do so now, go ahead and access a physical reminder of the younger creative passions you explored internally (and if this brings up too much fear or resistance, consider how you can gently dip your toe in). This might mean reading a book or watching a movie you loved as a child, or pulling out an old piece of artwork or some packed away sports equipment. Find something in your physical world that will allow you to tangibly experience the inspiration and creative feelings that this exercise brought up. It might be writing a single line of poetry, singing a line of a familiar song, or manifesting a small-form movement, idea, or creative technique. Simply explore the thoughts, feelings, and movements that come to you without any particular expectations.

Step 7. When you feel complete, sit down again and take a short moment of reflection. Visualize a short dream for yourself, where you see yourself creating and exploring in a completely free, joyful, uninhibited way. What if that experience were a part of a typical day for you in your life? How might the day look, or week unfold? You may wish to journal and write down some of what is coming to you. When you are ready, gently bring yourself back, letting yourself feel refreshed and complete in this moment.

My clients love this exploratory exercise! It might just guide you to rediscover a form of creative expression that once brought you joy—and can bring you joy again!

Helping others rediscover the childlike joy creative expression can bring is my mission… and, thanks to the power of leverage, I've been able to do it on a much larger scale.

If you're considering creating leverage in your business, I want you to know that you have all the knowledge and skills you need to begin. You *are* capable. Trust that you have the expertise and experience you need to begin right now.

I'm proof it's possible—I wasn't sure I could effectively do the work I do with people in a group setting or harness the Internet to teach piano. But I did!

Also, your first program doesn't have to be complicated; it doesn't have to include everything you know. It can focus on just one aspect of your expertise… something you know your people need. It's a wonderful way to deliver the expertise you've earned over the years as part of your first program.

If you're considering offering your services in a more leveraged way, my advice is to get clear on your unique gifts, your ideal audience, and the most effective entry point into your world for the members of that audience.

Then, design your course strategically with the proper guidance and support. After that, you can branch out and offer the full array of your services to clients through additional programs and offers.

And do take things one small step at a time. Yes, there's a lot to learn, but it's manageable if you sequence it properly. Plus, I promise it will give you a huge boost in confidence in yourself, your value, and your abilities—it's definitely done that for me.

Once you've begun your journey, I am also confident you'll be able to enjoy the rewards of leverage (more free time and a higher income), while helping a greater number of people... and experiencing the joy that comes from changing the world!

***

Sam Whitesell is the creator of the online piano program for adults, Back To The Piano: Play It Again With Sam! He began taking piano lessons at age six and now has 30 years of piano playing under his belt. With two university degrees in piano, 20 years' experience performing professionally in myriad styles and situations, and 15 years' experience teaching piano along the way, Sam's passion today is supporting adults who used to play in joyfully jumpstarting their playing again and deepening their connection with their powerful creative selves. Sam lives in Burlington, Vermont, U.S., on the banks of beautiful Lake Champlain, where he feels blessed to have the opportunity to revel daily in the surrounding natural splendor of the region and to be part of the wonderful local community. He performs regularly as pianist at the First Unitarian Society of Burlington, Vermont. Visit Sam online (and hear some of his music!) at www.SamuelWhitesell.com.

Get Sam's free gift ...

The Unleash Your Creativity! mini-course to reconnect with your inner creative spark and discover your creative outlet, here:

LeverageYourExpertiseBook.com/gifts

Leverage Your Expertise

Chapter 15
Dancing Through Life
by Melanie Dale

My Inspiration

My parents inspired me to be a dancer. I remember waking up to the music of Glenn Miller and Count Basie and watching dancing showcases on variety shows like *Jackie Gleason, Laurence Welk,* and *Ed Sullivan.* I also remember watching my parents' love demonstrated through dance.

I learned to dance as one learns language—in response to the sounds and movements of my childhood.

A Little Girl "Drummin' for Tobacco"

I feel like I have been an entrepreneur my entire life! My father was a tobacconist and taught me how to create and nurture business relationships when I was young. We used to go "drummin' tobacco" before I could even see over a steering wheel. He would set me in his lap and let me steer the car down the country roads as we visited the farmers and coaxed them into letting us sell their crop.

As a teenager, I knew most of the local farmers and could cover almost all of the jobs in the warehouse, including picking up the sale and calculating the farmer's pay.

Learning the Steps and Following the Music

Although talented in other art forms, dance was my favorite form of expression. I started ballet and tap lessons at the age of three, and by junior high, I could choreograph ballets to the music in my head. My destiny became clear to me in the seventh grade, when I wrote an autobiography that declared my intent to be a mother, dance teacher, and business owner.

To test the reality of this dream, I took a year away from my ballet major in college to start my own dance school, in which I taught ballet, tap, jazz, and disco to children and adults in the small tobacco town I knew so well.

Teaching dance was my destiny! After attending a summer workshop in Savannah, Georgia, I was invited to dance with the ballet company there under the direction of Karina Brock (ballerina), and I later became the dance director for the City of Savannah. I also registered in business classes at Savannah State College, and studied sales, basic computer programming, business communications, and accounting.

Beginning My Career

Little did I know that my job in Savannah would lead me to the ballroom dance business! While I was heading a dance project on the river front in Savannah, I met Cathy and Forrest, who persuaded me to join their teacher training program. I quickly became certified with the Fred Astaire organization.

Two years into my ballroom career, I married an International-style 10-Dance Champion, and we had a ballroom business in Florida. Unfortunately, despite our shared love of dance, fishing, golf, and music, alcoholism reigned over our marriage. As a single mother, I chose to open my own ballroom and later moved my business back to my home state of North Carolina.

My daughter inherited my love of the arts, and her passion for dancing, singing, and theatre classes, combined with my teaching duties, resulted in my traveling about 600 miles a week in my car. I was building my tribe the old-fashioned way, running from one community high school to another, as well as to private clubs and big companies, to teach ballroom dance.

Signing the Lease

After eight years of running a brick-and-mortar business in a small town outside of Raleigh, it became clear to me that I needed a storefront in Raleigh. I wanted to create a space for the dance community to learn and practice on a regular basis. It became a true labor of love—my students even helped me paint the walls and install the dance floor.

My rent also went up 12 times! Ouch! It was a huge leap of faith—so much so that my nerves caused eczema as my body reacted to the stress.

Despite many life challenges, I have applied my dance skills and business experiences to start and manage successful ballroom businesses for the last 38 years. I have owned and operated A Step to Gold International ballroom, a 5000-square-foot facility in Raleigh, N.C., for over 18 years now.

An Age-Old Problem

A few years ago, several of the ballroom regulars began experiencing health problems. They were undergoing back surgeries and knee/hip replacements, or suffering from pneumonia, cancer, and heart attacks.

Their absence in classes drastically affected my income. Most of my remaining in-person students were males or couples who had been taking lessons from me for over 10 years—since they were in their 60s.

Finding Mr. Ballroom

Replacing students proved difficult, so I needed to hire an advanced teacher to offer more compelling lessons and be a competition partner for female students.

Eric just happened to show up when I needed him most (I believe good things happen at the right time when you have faith!). He was a dream come true: hard-working, great-looking, fantastic customer service, high professionalism, and a talented dancer. Plus, we got along famously! I could not ask for more. We organized competitions and traveled to take our students to others, and we had some of the best parties in town! I felt confident that I would eventually be able to retire and leave the business to him.

That confidence disappeared the day Eric came to me and said he and his family were going to be deported to Belgium. His visa wouldn't allow him to stay in America, even though his mother lived in Raleigh. Unfortunately, he had let his citizenship go after he married a Belgium girl.

The students cried. I cried. And in two weeks, he was gone, leaving behind a big void in the ballroom.

Shuffle and Repeat

About that time, another instructor came along. I had known his younger brother and believed him to be honest and ethical. However, time proved that he was not a team player, and he was taking my newer students somewhere else to teach. He was offering them lower prices and swooning them. He had even signed a non-compete agreement with me but was clearly only looking after himself.

The next replacement was an excellent teacher, but I had to fire him when I found out he had a drug problem.

Moving on, I hired a teacher I had been acquainted with for several years. Needless to say, he disappointed me when he asked a student on a date and was telling other students he could take them to competitions a lot "cheaper" than I could.

Next, I flew in a teacher from Florida to audition for the job, but we didn't click. In retrospect, the cost to fly him in on a regular basis would have been unsustainable, anyhow.

Desperate, I called a friend of mine, Betty Lou, in Virginia Beach (which is over three hours away). She owned a ballroom and had hired several teachers from other countries, and recommended Riccardo, a 5'3" Italian 10-Dance Champion. I could not imagine him dancing with my tall ladies, but I set my doubts aside and had him come in for a trial. I knew his knowledge would be invaluable, but I didn't know how much the ladies would love him! He was cute, funny, and a great teacher and event planner. After a few days, they really didn't care how short he was. I think he stretched six inches when he danced! And he made them feel beautiful.

Riccardo could only give me two days a week, so I was on my sixth hire when COVID-19 hit. The pandemic magnified the social isolation which already existed across many age groups due to reliance on social media to find friendship and community.

In a way, it was also a Godsend. I couldn't keep doing the majority of in-person teaching. There was no one trained in the local area I could trust, and I needed a break!

Just Keep Dancing, Dancing, Dancing

"Nothing in this world can take the place of persistence. Talent will not; nothing is more common than unsuccessful men with talent. Genius will not; unrewarded genius is almost a proverb. Education will not; the world is full of educated derelicts. Persistence and determination alone are omnipotent." - Calvin Coolidge

My father always said, *"Hard work never hurt anybody. If things aren't the way you like it, do something about it."* That "something" was pivoting my business.

I decided to take it one day and one task at a time with Alina Vincent's Fast, Easy and Profitable Online Challenges course. It got me into action like I never imagined!

After running my 5-Day Challenge, Dance to Romance, I added 140 people to my email list and had about 50 in my private group, Dance For Couples. I was building a new tribe, and it felt good!

Before Christmas, I held a three-hour Pre-Holiday Ballroom Dance Workshop, based on the elements I taught in the Challenge. I had four participants, one of whom then enrolled in my **Master the Slow Dance** pilot program.

I also took some of the lessons from my Challenge and bundled them into a giveaway bundle called "Master the Elements of Social Dance." Being involved in the giveaway gave me experience being interviewed on Facebook and introduced me to other creative minds who were experiencing similar challenges in their businesses.

Now, I use parts of "Master the Elements of Social Dance" with new clients as an added bonus, to prepare them for continuing after the first lessons and in place of live group classes. And, I have a Challenge that I can run over and over that leads to my dance programs.

In February, I created my first online program, **Master the Slow Dance** (which included "Master the Elements of Social Dance" as a bonus).

And with Alina's help, I created a funnel, which is a way for people to find your product and follow various hyperlinks to become customers or refer others to your website. Her proven ideas for marketing without spending much (or any) money are so creative and doable. And she also shows you how to create workshops and other ways to bring in money with parts of your program.

Not only do I love being able to leverage my work this way, but it's been so helpful for new students—including those who are uncomfortable with in-person instruction, and especially those who do not like to be seen in person out of fear of "looking like a fool."

When the pandemic hit, I tried not to second-guess what *could* happen to my business. I never considered closing, even though I did not know how I was going to make the rent. Instead, I kept serving my customers through virtual lessons and working on my virtual programs.

Riccardo is still with me, teaching in person or virtually, every week. For my students, having both options has been perfect. Some of them go in and practice in-person with social distancing. It has kept them from getting depressed or out of shape, because they can interact in their little practice group that meets three days a week. Others who aren't comfortable being in person attend virtually.

Everything I do virtually is an asset to add value to my programs in person and online. I can use them in part or whole to supplement other programs I am selling.

I also think my current students have a new-found respect for me. They see how positive I am, and that I have a renewed interest in teaching and growing my business. Sometimes, you don't feel appreciated by students who have been around for a long time ... they tend to take you for granted. It feels good to be recognized!

One of my online students from Canada wrote:

"He [Heather's husband] hates dancing, to put it bluntly. He's so uncomfortable when you ask him to dance. So, he will, with me, preferably alone and with the lights out. He did get on a dance floor with me at one point. But when I went to reach for his hand, it was stiff at his side, and I was like, 'Okay, we're done!'

"[With Melanie], he picked it up! I'm so impressed. The first night, we did the "It's All in the Knees" video, and we practiced for half an hour. By the end of it, he was moving me around the room. I knew where he wanted me to go from his knees. He was a little sore afterward, but was also so excited about it. We're having fun; we're laughing our way through it. He's actually enjoying it!" - Heather Abbott

If you're smiling right now at the thought of dancing around your house with your significant other, I'd love for you to try the following exercise! It's the one Heather describes above, and it will boost your confidence while you have fun!

Exercise: Slow Dance Tonight: It's All in the Knees!

Step 1: Stand three inches apart from your partner (or the wall, if you don't have a partner), and bend your knees until they touch the wall or intertwine with your partner's. Repeat several times, straightening and bending without affecting your upper body posture.

Step 2: Practice bending your knees and moving them left and right by yourself, rolling to the inside edge of the free foot and allowing the hip to swing to the side.

Step 3: Practice Step 2 with your partner. Remember to keep knees alternating (follower on right side). Your right feet should be pointed between each other's feet.

Step 4: Continue the exercise, alternating from slow to fast rhythms with music.

Step 5: Rotate the movement left and right.

You are dancing!

This exercise demonstrates how teaching a foundational building block can engage and inspire people to want to learn. Regardless of the topic, identifying and disseminating the foundational building blocks will keep your students wanting more!

Creating and running online programs made me realize the immense value of the knowledge and experience I have to offer. It gave me a boost of confidence knowing that I can help people from all walks of life enjoy the benefits of dancing and bring back the spark in their relationships.

I now see myself able to influence many more people for years to come after I retire with my online programs.

What I've Learned

First and foremost, creating an online program with a mastermind of other people has inspired me to keep pushing forward in my business!

I've also learned that you can't depend 100% on others. Good employees are hard to find, and I never want to feel like my life is at the mercy of employees again. The only way to make a good living is by creating products (duplicating yourself) and learning how to market those programs.

I will never try to be something I am not. I was born to dance and have lived my dream my whole life. Now is the time to share to the world the tips and tricks of learning ballroom dance and reap the rewards of helping others experience magical moments through dance. That will only be possible with my online programs!

Some people think retirement begins in your sixties. I think my life is just beginning! Teaching lights me up, and I am loving teaching online!

I can't wait to be able to afford to take time off to go on a dance cruise, just for me, as a passenger as I profit from the leverage I have incorporated into my business.

My Advice for Leveraging with an Online Program

Big picture:

- Experience is the best teacher. Try and experience everything for which you have time. Run the workshops, challenges, and VIP days. And acknowledge yourself for small wins. We need to celebrate ourselves as much as we can instead of focusing on our failures … which is something I tell my students all the time.

- People respond to your mistakes the same way you do. They want to see you succeed, and if you are nervous and upset, they will be nervous and upset, too. Don't give them the opportunity to feel bad for you, no matter what happens. Keep smiling! A smile goes a long way. It relieves you and them.

- Give yourself permission to fail and keep going! Even in sales, remind yourself that behind every "No," there is a "Yes!" We do the best we can, and that's all we can do!

More specifically:

- If you have another job or brick-and-mortar business like me, invest in a virtual or in-person assistant to do some of the busy work for you, like sending emails or editing videos and creating Facebook ads.

- My assistant is a college student majoring in marketing. We work three days a week and bounce ideas off each other for about four hours each day. She has been such a big help with the busy work and technical side of things.

- I am beginning to think I need a virtual assistant, too, now that things are picking up at the ballroom!

- And one more thing… keep trying.

***

LeverageYourExpertiseBook.com/gifts

Melanie Dale has over 38 years of experience in the ballroom dance business. She has trained professionals and has an extensive background in American and International styles of ballroom dancing, having been trained by many of the GREATS from Europe and the US, including her former husband, the legendary Larry Silvers, who was the first United States Professional Ballroom Champion. Melanie has seen students transform their lives through ballroom dance on and off the dance floor. "Melanie is a terrific teacher who cares about people. and who sincerely gives 100% of herself to the art of ballroom dancing."- Dance Critic and Founder of Dance Beat Magazine, Didio Barrera. You can learn more about her here: ballroomdancementor.com.

Get Melanie's free gift …

Slow Dance Tonight: It's All in the Knees!
to discover the secret to connecting to your partner for leading and following in social dance, here:

LeverageYourExpertiseBook.com/gifts

Chapter 16
You're One Action Away from Changing Your Life
by Sidra Gaines

Twenty years ago, when my daughter was young, she wanted so much to go to camp. As a single mom, I just couldn't afford it… but I really wanted to. I felt horrible telling her I couldn't swing it, financially.

So I took action: I scoured the Internet looking for ways to make the extra money. I discovered that people were earning quite a bit by selling products online. After buying and pouring over multiple eBooks and courses, I realized that, since I did not have a lot of money, I would have to find inexpensive items to sell for significantly more than I'd bought them for in order to turn a decent profit.

The math was simple, but I definitely had to come up with a process for successfully putting the concept into action.

I'll never forget my first sale: I sold an eight-dollar calculator I had sitting in a drawer for $42.00. Over the next few weeks, I sold more and more. I paid for my daughter's camp and covered several other major expenses, as well.

I've since spent thousands of dollars and dozens of hours on trainings to help me create a simple, predictable model for generating consistent income by selling on Amazon.

As my daughter grew older, the money I made selling items online paid for her to participate in sports in high school and go to college. Later, I had enough to begin paying my 93-year-old mother's house payment and allow my 27-year-old daughter who has mental health challenges to live independently.

I'm so grateful I learned this incredible skill! **Not only has it empowered me financially, but it's brought out the entrepreneur hidden inside a previously risk-averse person.**

Selling items online was so life-changing for me that I began teaching others how to do it, too. And it was so rewarding!

I started with my friends, and with each friend, I spent hours taking him or her through the steps to learn to sell online. I noticed I didn't have time to cover each step as deeply and thoroughly as I would have liked, though.

Creating a course to reach more people—and change more lives—seemed like a natural next step not only because I spent an inordinate amount of time training people individually, but also because I could teach each skill more deeply. Also, if I'm being totally transparent, I saw them creating a significant income and thought, "Hmm, could I charge them for this training?!" In fact, a couple of people offered me money to provide more training, but I just didn't have the time.

Although offering an online course was always on my mind, I didn't take consistent, focused action to actually do it. I, like most entrepreneurs, have a lot on my plate: I'm a school administrator, I take care of my mother, and I am helping my young adult daughter set out in life.

Focusing on my own dreams, desires, and passions just wasn't a priority.

Fortunately, six months ago, I joined Alina's Rising Stars Mastermind, and she and her team supported me to take action and create a true course. Honestly, it would have taken me so long to do it otherwise (if ever!). I'd toyed with the idea of creating a course, but life kept getting in the way.

During the process of creating my first course, **Sell Online Like A Pro** (a five-week program that takes people from signing up on Amazon to getting their first shipment out the door), I realized I have the crucial information inside of me to support people in creating six-figure businesses.

While I felt overwhelmed with the idea of creating an entire course, I wanted to meet my clients' needs. So, I ran weekly 90-minute Q&A sessions throughout my course, too. What I didn't expect was the realization of how much knowledge

I actually had— I was not at a loss for answers. I never got stumped!

Plus, it's about so much more than just selling; it's about the techniques required to sell like a professional—maximizing people's ability to create a life-changing income.

Case in point: The first time I offered the program, 18 people enrolled, and I made more than $5,000.

By its very nature, Sell Online Like A Pro *is* leverage. It has allowed me to reach more people by leveraging my time and resources, and it's also allowed me to leverage my personal knowledge ... I've now brought into the light vast stores of intellectual resources I didn't even realize I had. My influence has increased exponentially!

I've also learned some important lessons: for example, as much as I love one-on-one interaction, it's not the best way to impart deep knowledge; I also discovered that I have a strong base of influence on Facebook that easily translated into my followers trusting my ability to support them in learning to sell on Amazon.

And now, I am looking forward to developing even more leverage through different tools like 5-Day Facebook Challenges and a Facebook group, which will help me reach people who don't already know me.

It's now my mission to teach people a skill that will make them money and allow them to live their purpose and dreams. And based on my clients' experiences so far, it's working!

One of the stories that touches me deeply is that of Ann and her son, a bright young man who experienced severe trauma and was unable to leave the home. For years, Ann struggled to find a way for him to experience success in life. She enrolled in Sell Online Like A Pro, and she and her son completed it together. He's now on his way to building a successful business! Even more importantly, Ann excitedly shared with me that she can see the light in his eyes has been reignited; he feels happy and productive again.

This is the greatest gift I've received from creating an online course: helping other people achieve their goals and seeing their lives change (and my increased income is a welcome bonus!).

It means so much to be to help other people achieve their goals and change their lives.

To give you a taste of what I do, I'd like to share an exercise with you.

Many people don't realize how many things (new and used) they have at home right this second that they could sell on Amazon and start earning money right now. Complete this exercise to get a feel for what items of your own you might have.

Exercise: The "Got Profit?" Amazon Treasure Hunt

Step 1. Get on Amazon.com, and spend a few minutes exploring what's for sale in lots of different categories (food, electronics, hardware, books, toys/games, housewares, etc.).

Step 2. Go through your home and garage and identify items you'd be willing to sell.

Step 3. Get back on Amazon and search for those same items, so you can see what your "treasure" is worth.

Step 4. Once you find 10 items that you're willing to sell *and* that are listed on Amazon, use the Amazon Fee Calculator to see how much you could make if you sold your items there.

Just like that, you can see how there is lots of income hidden in plain sight when you sell things of your own that you don't need. Imagine the unwanted items you might sell if you asked your friends and neighbors to donate, or if you started going to garage sales!

If you enjoy this exercise, selling on Amazon might be perfect for you!

Whether you're looking for a hobby, or need additional income quickly, you *can* create a better world for yourself. And as I mentioned earlier, the absolute best part of my success hasn't been monetary (although I've loved the income!). It's been providing others the information and inspiration to do just that.

If there's one thing I'd love for you to take away from reading my story, it's this:

I waited 20 years to create my course. I missed 20 years of helping people make more money and change their lives. I can't even imagine how much money I would have made had I launched my course 20 years ago. The sad part is, I didn't need any more knowledge or expertise—I already had it within me. What I did need was the willingness to make myself and my dreams a priority.

You CAN take action today to change your life and that of your family by manifesting the very things you have only dreamt about until now.

You've got this!

***

Sidra Gaines has been a lifelong entrepreneur trapped in the body of a risk-averse woman. It was only after she invested in a mentor that she began living her dreams and supporting the dreams of others by creating Sell Online Like A Pro, which helps beginners create a lifestyle business. She has an incredible 93-year-old mother and a powerhouse of a young adult daughter. You can learn more about Sidra and her course here: www.sellonlinelikeapro.com.

Get Sidra's free gift ...

Where To Find Free and Low-Cost Items To Sell On Amazon to help you find even more items to sell for great profits, here:

LeverageYourExpertiseBook.com/gifts

Chapter 17
Always Go with Your Gut
by Christine Grauer

Mousie.

That was my name, according to my family and close friends… until I was around 40 years old. You see, as a little girl, I wanted to escape the signs of violence in my home: broken glass, bullet holes in furniture, black eyes, and swollen, bloody lips. I constantly hid to avoid confrontation and getting black eyes myself. So, I could usually be found behind the curtains or under the bed.

Hence, the nickname. It was my strategy for staying safe.

The only thing was, I kept using that strategy well into adulthood, despite not having any need to. Because I was a capable adult.

On the outside.

But on the inside, I continued to silence my voice and run from conflict. And with an emotionally, verbally, mentally, and sexually abusive partner, repressing my voice and standing up for myself only exacerbated the anguish I felt inside. It affected the way I parented. It stifled my joy and vitality. And it led to life-threatening illness.

A month after recovering from sepsis from a ruptured appendix, *I decided to leap through fear*. I ended that toxic relationship of ten years and became a single mom (again) to my two children.

Mere months after that leap, pieces of my purpose started falling into my lap. Funny how that happens.

I had been fervently and intently studying spirituality for about 12 years, and I knew that there was more to life than my five senses were telling me. So, when a program for spiritual life coach certification appeared in my path, I signed up and went $10k into debt (further, that is, than I was already) without hesitation.

My mind fretted over the decision, but my heart simply knew. There was no denying that this was the program for me.

You know when you know.

As I continued to say "YES" to opportunities that organically fell into my path and lured me to step out of my comfort zone, the more aligned I felt with my true calling. I then invested thousands of dollars more to get my Energy Codes® Facilitator Certification. Another strong "YES" that I simply couldn't deny.

In the meantime, despite ending my toxic relationship and finally feeling a deep passion and inner knowing of my life's purpose, life outside of me was a whirlwind. I was tasked with fighting my ex through years of messy court battles over support and custody of our daughter.

The even greater challenge, however, was dealing with my son's aggressive behavior in the home: a by-product of mental health issues that developed through marijuana use. So, again, I was faced with standing up for myself and enforcing my personal boundaries, not only in response to threats and verbal abuse from my ex, but also from my own son.

But through the support of my own life coach and my spiritual mentor, coupled with the intense training I was completing through my coaching certifications, I developed systems that not only broke through my dysfunctional Mousie subconscious beliefs and patterns, but also upgraded my parenting skills.

I developed a parenting system that leveraged my knowledge of *science* through my master's degree, *spirituality* from decades of studying and the mentoring and training I had received, and *psychology* from my spiritual life coach training.

And thanks to my teenagers, I was presented with one opportunity after another to apply and refine this parenting system!

After firmly setting boundaries with my ex and my son, I began to focus on following my passion. I registered my business as "**Christine Grauer**," built a website, and began helping women get amazing results through private coaching.

The next order of business was writing the teaching memoir that was burning inside of me. After an incredible 18-month journey of writing, *Project: LIFE – Stop Waiting for Your Happy to Happen* was birthed and released to the world.

Shortly after my book launched, I came across Alina's Rising Stars Mastermind. Another big investment. More debt. Gulp.

Funny enough, a week prior to Alina's invitation to her program, I had pre-recorded a video to post on social media. As I listened to it, I heard myself tell my audience to step through fear and ignore the fear-based voice of their inner naysayer… the one that comes up with repeated excuses. In the end, my final advice was, "Always go with your gut."

It felt like my future self was talking to me. And as a coach who walked her talk, I couldn't *not* take this plunge. With tears of excitement, relief, and fear, I said "YES" again!

And here I am.

Thanks to Alina's work, I now have a solid online program—Harmony Secrets for Moms of Teens—that's providing incredible results for moms of teenagers.

What I didn't mention earlier is that the way I had parented my son contributed to his mental health issues. I made many mistakes, because I simply wasn't equipped to handle the extreme challenges I faced with him. And because of those experiences, I hold every mom and every teenager close to my heart. I've seen the severe struggles that my own teens have gone through, and how my every word and action has either helped or hindered their personal growth and self-esteem. I know how greatly our teens struggle and what they need from us, as their moms, to help get them back on track.

I compassionately relate to what moms everywhere are going through—I've *been* the struggling and frustrated mom who wants to scream, run away, cry, and give up… but in the same breath, also love and support my teens. (OMG.)

Through my tried-and-proven system, dozens of moms have found peace of mind and harmony in their home. And without the power of leveraging my online program, I wouldn't be able to support the number of moms that I do today. Prior to my program, I was only coaching students one-on-one, and it was incredibly time intensive... especially as a single mom working full-time and looking after an older home. My days went from about 6 a.m. to midnight to make it all happen.

Despite the excessive time I invested in coaching women in my "free time," I was leery about creating an online program in the hopes of leveraging my precious time. I mean, how on Earth could moms get results from watching something online? They needed *me* to coach them! They needed to interact with me to make transformational shifts in their lives!

But after listening to Alina explain how to create an online program, I was sold. I dove right in! Within two months of completing her High Profit Programs event and signing up for Rising Stars Mastermind, I released the pilot version of Harmony Secrets for Moms of Teens.

My biggest realization that swayed me into taking this particular leap in creating the online program was that I had several core teachings and practices that I repeated with each of my students—information that was foundational and vital to my students' ability to create the changes they desired. So, I isolated the foundational teachings and practices, and they formed the core of Harmony Secrets.

By that process alone, I leveraged countless hours of my time that would have been spent with each student repeating the same information to them in our private sessions. As an adult educator and instructional designer, I have over twenty years of experience in creating programs and online courses. So, leveraging my course design skills and software helped me whip up my online program with little ramp-up time!

On the other hand, website development wasn't something I did regularly, nor had I any time to learn it! So, I invested in a reliable web-designer/developer, and she performed the bulk of the changes needed on my website and mail-client to get my program setup. It was far better use of my time to focus on the things that came naturally and easily for me than to spend it on things in which I was not proficient.

Now that I have my online program, very little of my time is required to deliver potent and essential information to the people who need it! When my private coaching students take Harmony Secrets before I coach them, we are then able to delve deeper into their individualized program from the start. Not only does this leverage my time, but it saves my students money!

When I had discovered my passion and purpose as a life coach, I also revealed a love of connecting with people. So, I made dozens and dozens of beautiful and meaningful connections with other coaches and influencers in my community as well as globally. And now that I have an online program, I can also leverage these relationships through affiliate partnerships! It's a win-win-win scenario: less of my time spent marketing and gathering potential students; my partners are compensated with a percentage of sales earned from Harmony Secrets; and the lives of moms and their teens are shifting in beautiful ways, just like Inna's:

Inna, a single mom, was in a desperate state when she started my program. She was crying almost every day and constantly fighting to get her teen daughter to get pick up after herself and do chores around the home.

After the program, not only did Inna notice a shift in herself and in her relationship with her daughter, but her daughter commented on how calm Inna had become. The fights stopped! Although the daughter didn't always do what she was asked, the relationship had blossomed into one where the daughter felt comfortable confiding in her mom. The level of trust increased, the communication opened, and, on occasion, her daughter even helped around the home without being asked!

One of the key methods I taught Inna was to approach her daughter from an emotionally neutral state—because when we engage in any interaction from an emotionally charged state, we increase the chance of our teen resisting us and our message!

So how the heck do we do that?

It's quite simple. Not necessarily easy… especially in the heat of an emotional trigger… but *simple*.

Exercise: Stay Calm, Cool, and Connected Despite Having a Teen

Here's an overview of the steps to release an emotional charge, so you can approach situations in a calm and connected manner (by the way, this applies to *any* interaction, not just those with your teen):

Step 1: The moment you get activated, diffuse the emotional charge in your body with an immediate and aggressive exhale through the mouth. Even if there's nothing left in the lungs—exhale. Completely. Let it out. Add some sound, if it feels good.

Step 2: When possible, remove yourself from the situation. Resist the urge to snap back and defend yourself. Bite your tongue. Simply walk away.

Step 3: Sit or stand with a straight spine, and let the next inhale be through the nose. It should be deep and slow. Your belly should expand fully. Visualize white light coming into your body as you do this.

Step 4: Let the exhale be assertive and through the mouth. With it, visualize heavy, dark clouds of energy being released through your mouth or belly button, whichever feels intuitively right for you.

Step 5: Repeat this style of breathing for a few cycles until the strong energy charge is diffused. You'll feel when it happens.

Communicating from an emotionally neutral state is the best way to have our message be heard and better received. If you follow these simple steps with persistence and consistency, you'll find you're better able to approach challenging situations with a calm and centered approach.

This will come in handy when you choose to scale and leverage your business by creating an online program, too… which, in my experience, is the quickest and easiest way to do so!

Working with clients one-on-one is great, but we have amazing things to share with people—and more people than those we can reach individually need our help! With an online program, your reach is limitless. Plus, it's more financially accessible than one-on-one coaching for those who need it.

If you're about to embark on the online course-creation journey (you're going to love it!), I have some final suggestions from the lessons I've learned:

First, remember that "less is more." I tried to compress far too much information into the pilot version of my program. Despite hearing it at least a dozen times, I still put too much information into it, because as an expert in my domain, I wanted to give as much as I could to moms. But information overload is a real thing. Next time around, I will stick to the bare essential information!

Second, simply take action.

We're all busy and overwhelmed at times, but when we want something bad enough, and it aligns with our deeper purpose (it just *feels* right), then it'll happen if we commit and take action!

Finally, say "YES" to life!

Regardless of how scary it may seem, if it feels good and right in your heart and gut, go for it!

Without some huge and risky "YES"es in my life, I wouldn't be where I am today. Saying "YES" to creating an online program has been so beneficial. It's helped me gain credibility and authority. I have partners who want to promote my program. And I've effortlessly gained a wider reach! Plus, having an online program with proven results has helped people recognize me as an expert in my domain.

As a single mom working full-time, looking after a home, and running a coaching business, I've learned that time is absolutely our greatest treasure! Sure, saving money is great—but you can always get money back! Time, on the contrary, you cannot. So, leverage it wisely!

Much love to you!

***

Christine Grauer helps moms who feel like pulling out their hair or kicking their teenager/young adult out of the home to develop a more connected, meaningful, and respectful relationship with them. She is the author of the Amazon best-seller Project: LIFE – Stop Waiting for Your Happy to

Happen. Although she studied spirituality for over 20 years and earned a Master of Science Degree as well as Spiritual Life Coach and Energy Codes® Certifications, it was only through her past of loss, abuse, suffering, and illness that she could become the powerful and compassionate leader she is today. Through her elaborate studies and learning from trial and error while parenting her own teens, Christine developed a proven system that's rooted in science, spirituality, and psychology to help moms to stop feeling frustrated and worried about their teens and start enjoying a meaningful and connected relationship with them, like they used to when their kids were younger. She is a single mom of a teen, a young adult, and a chihuahua, and lives her passion-filled life of service in Waterloo, Ontario, Canada. You can learn more about her here: www.christinegrauer.com.

Get Christine's free gift …

Stay Calm, Cool, and Connected Despite Having a Teen, a quick-fix training for navigating emotional blow-ups that not only models leadership and love for your kids, but that keeps you focused and on track in your professional life here:

LeverageYourExpertiseBook.com/gifts

LeverageYourExpertiseBook.com/gifts

ABOUT Alina Vincent

Alina Vincent is a business strategist, speaker, and international bestselling author of the *Teach Your Expertise* book. She's known globally as the creator of the **High Profit Programs** blueprint and **5-Day Challenge Launch Formula** which helped her grow her business from zero to over a million dollars in just four years.

Alina is passionate about helping entrepreneurs package and monetize their knowledge and expertise to create a leveraged and scalable business. Experts hire her for strategic advice and a simple step-by-step approach to creating successful online programs, engaged Facebook communities, and profitable 5-Day Challenges.

Join her free Facebook group here:
facebook.com/groups/BusinessOwnersWhoThinkBig.

Leverage Your Expertise

LeverageYourExpertiseBook.com/gifts

BONUS GIFTS

This book comes with free gifts, exercises, and resources from each of the contributing authors.

You can access all of them on the bonus Resources Page:

LeverageYourExpertiseBook.com/gifts

Leverage Your Expertise

Made in the USA
Middletown, DE
31 August 2021